FAT AND BLOOD

S. Weir Mitchell

Contents

FAT AND BLOOD

BY

S. Weir Mitchell

PREFACE TO THE EIGHTH EDITION.

The continued favor which this book has enjoyed in Europe as well as in this country has rendered me doubly desirous to make it a thorough and clear statement of the treatment of the kind of cases which it discusses as carried out in my practice to-day.

In the endeavor to do this, the present edition, like the last two, has been carefully revised by my son, Dr. John K. Mitchell, and there is no chapter, and scarcely a page, where some alteration or addition has not been made, besides those of the sixth and seventh editions, as the result of added years of experience. Especially in the chapters on the means of treatment some details have been thought worth adding to help the statement so often repeated in the book that success will depend on the care with which details are carried out. The chapter on massage, rewritten for the last edition, has been once more revised and somewhat extended, in order to make it an accurate as well as a scientific, if brief, statement of the best method which use and observation have taught us. A chapter on the handling of several diseases not described in former editions has been added by the editor.

S. WEIR MITCHELL.

SEPTEMBER, 1899.

CHAPTER I.
INTRODUCTORY.

For some years I have been using with success, in private and in hospital practice, certain methods of renewing the vitality of feeble people by a combination of entire rest and excessive feeding, made possible by passive exercise obtained through the steady use of massage and electricity.

The cases thus treated have been chiefly women of a class well known to every physician,--nervous women, who, as a rule, are thin and lack blood. Most of them have been such as had passed through many hands and been treated in turn for gastric, spinal, or uterine troubles, but who remained at the end as at the beginning, invalids, unable to attend to the duties of life, and sources alike of discomfort to themselves and anxiety to others.

In 1875 I published in "Seguin's Series of American Clinical Lectures," Vol. I., No. iv., a brief sketch of this treatment, under the heading of "Rest in the Treatment of Nervous Disease," but the scope afforded me was too brief for the details on a knowledge of which depends success in the use of rest, I have been often since reminded of this by the many letters I have received asking for explanations of the minutiae of treatment; and this must be my apology for bringing into these pages a great many particulars which are no doubt well enough known to the more accomplished physician.

In the preface to the second edition I said that as yet there had been hardly time for a competent verdict on the methods I had described. Since making this statement, many of our profession in America have published cases of the use of my treatment. It has also been thoroughly discussed by the medical section of the British Medical Association, and warmly endorsed by William Playfair, of London, Ross of Manchester, Coghill, and others; while a translation of my book into French by Dr. Oscar Jennings, with an introduction by Professor Ball, and a reproduction in German, with a preface by Professor von Leyden, have placed it satisfactorily before the profession in France and Germany.

As regards the question of originality I did not and do not now much concern myself. This alone I care to know, that by the method in question cases are cured which once were not; and as to the novelty of the matter it would be needless to say more, were it not that the charge of lack of that quality is sometimes taken as an imputation on a man's good faith.

But to sustain so grave an implication the author must have somewhere laid claim to originality and said in what respect he considered himself to have done a totally new thing. The following passage from the first edition of this book explains what was my own position:

"I do not wish," I wrote, "to be thought of as putting forth anything very remarkable or original in my treatment by rest, systematic feeding, and passive exercise. All of these have been used by physicians; but, as a rule, one or more are used without the others, and the plan which I have found so valuable, of combining these means, does not seem to be generally understood. As it involves some novelty, and as I do not find it described elsewhere, I shall, I think, be doing a service to my profession by relating my experience."

The following quotation from Dr. William Playfair's essay[1] says all that I would care to add:

"The claims of Dr. Weir Mitchell to originality in the introduction of this system of treatment, which I have recently heard contested in more than one quarter, it is not my province to defend. I feel bound, however, to say that, having carefully studied what has been written on the subject, I can nowhere find anything in the least approaching to the regular, systematic, and thorough attack on the disease here discussed.

"Certain parts of the treatment have been separately advised, and more or less successfully practised, as, for example, massage and electricity, without isolation; or isolation and judicious moral management alone. It is, in fact, the old story with regard to all new things: there is no discovery, from the steam-engine down to chloroform, which cannot be shown to have been partially foreseen, and yet the claims of Watt and Simpson to originality remain practically uncontested. And so, if I may be permitted to compare small things with great, will it be with this. The whole matter was admirably summed up by Dr. Ross, of Manchester, in his remarks in the discussion I introduced at the meeting of the British Medical Association at Worcester, which I conceive to express the precise state of the case: 'Although Dr. Mitchell's treatment was not new in the sense that its separate recommendations were made for the first time, it was new in the sense that these recommendations were for the first time combined so as to form a complete scheme of treatment.'"

As regards the acceptance of this method of treatment I have to-day no complaint to make. It runs, indeed, the risk of being employed in cases which do not need it and by persons who are not competent, and of being thus in a measure brought into disrepute. As concerns one of its essentials--massage--this is especially to be feared. It is a remedy with capacity to hurt as well as to help, and should never be used without the advice of a physician, nor persistently kept up without medical observation of its temporary and more permanent effects.

CHAPTER II.
GAIN OR LOSS OF WEIGHT
CLINICALLY CONSIDERED.

The gentlemen who have done me the honor to follow my clinical service at the State Infirmary for Diseases of the Nervous System[2] are well aware how much care is there given to learn whether or not the patient is losing or has lost flesh, is by habit thin or fat. This question is one of the utmost moment in every point of view, and deserves a larger share of attention than it receives. In this hospital it is the custom to weigh our cases when they enter and at intervals. The mere loss of fat is probably of small moment in itself when the amount of restorative food is sufficient for every-day expenditure, and when the organs are in condition to keep up the supply of fat which we not only require for constant use but probably need to change continually. The steady or rapid lessening of the deposits of hydro-carbons stored away in the areolae of the tissues is of importance, as indicating their excessive use or a failure of supply; and when either condition is to be suspected it becomes our duty to learn the reasons for this striking symptom. Loss of flesh has also a collateral value of great import, because it is almost an invariable rule that rapid thinning is accompanied soon or late with more or less anaemia, and it is uncommon to see a person steadily gaining fat after any pathological reduction of weight without a corresponding gain in amount and quality of blood. We too rarely reflect that the blood thins with the decrease of the tissues and enriches as they increase.

Before entering into this question further, I shall ask attention to some points connected with the normal fat of the human body; and, taking for granted, here and elsewhere, that my readers are well enough aware of the physiological value and uses of the adipose tissues, I shall continue to look at the matter chiefly from a clinical point of view.

When in any individual the weight varies rapidly or slowly, it is nearly always due, for the most part, to a change in the amount of adipose tissue stored away in the meshes of the areolar tissue. Almost any grave change for the worse in health is at once betrayed in most people by a diminution of fat, and this is readily seen in the altered forms of the face, which, because it is the always visible and in outline the most irregular part of the body, shows first and most plainly the loss or gain of tissue. Fatty matter is therefore that constituent of the body which goes and comes most easily. Why there is in nearly every one a normal limit to its accumulation we cannot say, nor yet why this limit should vary as life goes on. Even in health the weight of men, and still more of women, is by no means constant, but, as a rule, when we are holding our own with that share of stored-up fat which belongs to the individual we are usually in a condition of nutritive prosperity, and when after any strain or trial which has lessened weight we are slowly repairing mischief and laying by fat we are equally in a state of health. The loss of fat which is not due to change of diet or to exercise, especially its rapid or steady loss, nearly always goes along with conditions which impoverish the blood, and, on the other hand, the gain of fat up to a certain point seems to go hand in hand with a rise in all other essentials of health, and notably with an improvement in the color and amount of the red corpuscles.

The quantity of fat which is healthy for the individual varies with the sex, the climate, the habits, the season, the time of life, the race, and the breed. Quetelet[3] has shown that before puberty the weight of the male is for equal ages above that of the female, but that towards puberty the proportional weight of the female, due chiefly to gain in fat, increases, so that at twelve the two sexes are alike in this respect. During the child-bearing time there is an absolute lessening on the part of the female, but after this time the weight of the woman increases, and the maximum is attained at about the age of fifty.

Dr. Henry I. Bowditch[4] reaches somewhat similar conclusions, and shows from much more numerous measurements of Boston children that growing boys are heavier in proportion to their height than girls until they reach fifty-eight inches, which is attained about the fourteenth year. Then the girl passes the boy in weight, which Dr. Bowditch thinks is due to the accumulation of adipose tissue at puberty. After two or three years more the male again acquires and retains superiority in weight and height.

Yet as life advances there are peculiarities which belong to individuals and to families. One group thins as life goes on past forty; another group as surely takes on flesh; and the same traits are often inherited, and are to be regarded when the question of fattening becomes of clinical or diagnostic moment. Men, as a rule, preserve their nutritive status more equably than women. Every physician must have been struck with this. In fact, many women lose or acquire large amounts of adipose matter without any corresponding loss or gain in vigor, and this fact perhaps is related in some way to the enormous outside demands made by their peculiar physiological processes. Such gain in weight is a common accompaniment of child-bearing, while nursing in some women involves considerable gain in flesh, and in a larger number enormous falling away, and its cessation as speedy a renewal of fat. I have also found that in many women who are not perfectly well there is a notable loss of weight at every menstrual period, and a marked gain between these times.

I was disappointed not to find this matter dealt with fully in Mrs. Jacobi's able essay on menstruation, nor can I discover elsewhere any observations in regard to loss or gain of weight at menstrual periods in the healthy woman.

How much influence the seasons have, is not as yet well understood, but in our own climate, with its great extremes, there are some interesting facts in this connection. The upper classes are with us in summer placed in the best conditions for increase in flesh, not only because it is their season of least work, mental and physical, but also because they are then for the most part living in the country under circumstances favorable to appetite, to exercise, and to freedom from care. Owing to these fortunate facts, members of the class in question are apt to gain weight in summer, although many such persons, as I know, follow the more general rule and lose weight. But if we deal with the mass of men who are hard worked, physically, and unable to leave the towns, we shall probably find that they nearly always lose weight in hot weather. Some support is given to this idea by the following very curious facts. Very many years ago I was engaged for certain purposes in determining the weight, height, and girth of all the members of our city police force. The examination was made in April and repeated in the beginning of October. Every care was taken to avoid errors, but to my surprise I found that a large majority of the men had lost weight during the summer. The sum total of loss was enormous. As I have mislaid some of the sheets, I am unable to give it accurately, but I found that three out of every five had lessened in weight. It would be interesting to know if such a change occurs in convicts confined in penitentiaries.

I am acquainted with some persons who lose weight in winter, and with more who fail in flesh in the spring, which is our season of greatest depression in health,-- the season when with us choreas are apt to originate[5] or to recur, and when habitual epileptic fits become more frequent in such as are the victims of that disease.

Climate has a good deal to do with a tendency to take on fat, and I think the first thing which strikes an American in England is the number of inordinately fat middle-aged people, and especially of fat women.

This excess of flesh we usually associate in idea with slothfulness, but English women exercise more than ours, and live in a land where few days forbid it, so that probably such a tendency to obesity is due chiefly to climatic causes. To these latter also we may no doubt ascribe the habits of the English as to food. They are larger feeders than we, and both sexes consume strong beer in a manner which would in this country be destructive of health. These habits aid, I suspect, in producing the more general fatness in middle and later life, and those enormous occasional growths which so amaze an American when first he sets foot in London. But, whatever be the cause, it is probable that members of the prosperous classes of English, over forty, would outweigh the average American of equal height of that period, and this must make, I should think, some difference in their relative liability to certain forms of disease, because the overweight of our trans-Atlantic cousins is plainly due to excess of fat.

I have sought in vain for English tables giving the weight of men and women of various heights at like ages. The material for such a study of men in America is given in Gould's researches published by the United States Sanitary Commission, and in Baxter's admirable report,[6] but is lacking for women. A comparison of these points as between English and Americans of both sexes would be of great interest.

I doubt whether in this country as notable a growth in bulk as multitudes of English attain would be either healthy or desirable in point of comfort, owing to the distress which stout people feel in our hot summer weather. Certainly "Banting" is with us a rarely-needed process, and, as a rule, we have much more frequent occasion to fatten than to thin our patients. The climatic peculiarities which have changed our voices, sharpened our features, and made small the American hand and foot, have also made us, in middle and advanced life, a thinner and more sallow race, and, possibly, adapted us better to the region in which we live. The same changes in form are in like manner showing themselves in the English race in Australia.[7]

Some gain in flesh as life goes on is a frequent thing here as elsewhere, and usually has no unwholesome meaning. Occasionally we see people past the age of sixty suddenly taking on fat and becoming at once unwieldy and feeble, the fat collecting in masses about the belly and around the joints. Such an increase is sometimes accompanied with fatty degeneration of the heart and muscles, and with a certain watery flabbiness in the limbs, which, however, do not pit on pressure.

Alcoholism also gives rise in some people to a vast increase of adipose tissue, and the sodden, unwholesome fatness of the hard drinker is a sufficiently well known and unpleasant spectacle. The overgrowth of inert people who do not exercise enough to use up a healthy amount of overfed tissues is common enough as an individual peculiarity, but there are also two other conditions in which fat is apt to be accumulated to an uncomfortable extent. Thus, in some cases of hysteria where the patient lies abed owing to her belief that she is unable to move about, she is apt in time to become enormously stout. This seems to me also to be favored by the large use of morphia to which such women are prone, so that I should say that long rest, the hysterical constitution, and the accompanying resort to morphia make up a group of conditions highly favorable to increase of fat.

Lastly, there is the class of fat anaemic people, usually women. This double peculiarity is rather uncommon, but, as the mass of thin-blooded persons are as a rule thin or losing flesh, there must be something unusual in that anaemia which goes with gain in flesh.

Bauer[8] thinks that lessened number of blood-corpuscles gives rise to storing of fat, owing to lessened tissue-combustion. At all events, the absorption of oxygen diminishes after bleeding, and it used to be well known that some people grew fat when bled at intervals. Also, it is said that cattle-breeders in some localities--certainly not in this country--bleed their cattle to cause increase of fat in the tissues, or

of fat secreted as butter in the milk. These explanations aid us but little to comprehend what, after all, is only met with in certain persons, and must therefore involve
conditions not common to every one who is anaemic. Meanwhile, the group of fat
anaemics is of the utmost clinical interest, as I shall by and by point out more distinctly.

There is a popular idea, which has probably passed from the agriculturist into
the common mind of the community, to the effect that human fat varies,--that
some fat is wholesome and some unwholesome, that there are good fats and bad
fats. I remember well an old nurse who assured me when I was a student that "some
fats is fast and some is fickle, but cod-oil fat is easy squandered."

There are more facts in favor of some such idea than I have place for, but as
yet we have no distinct chemical knowledge as to whether the fats put on under
alcohol or morphia, or rapidly by the use of oils, or pathologically in fatty degenerations, or in anaemia, vary in their constituents. It is not at all unlikely that such is
the case, and that, for example, the fat of an obese anaemic person may differ from
that of a fat and florid person. The flabby, relaxed state of many fat people is possibly due not alone to peculiarities of the fat, but also to want of tone and tension in
the areolar tissues, which, from all that we now know of them, may be capable of
undergoing changes as marked as those of muscles.

That, however, animals may take on fat which varies in character is well known
to breeders of cattle. "The art of breeding and feeding stock," says Dr. Letheby,[9]
"is to overcome excessive tendency to accumulation of either surface fat or visceral
fat, and at the same time to produce a fat which will not melt or boil away in cooking. Oily foods have a tendency to make soft fats which will not bear cooking." Such
differences are also seen between English and American bacon, the former being
much more solid; and we know, also, that the fat of different animals varies remarkably, and that some, as the fat of hay-fed horses, is readily worked off. Such facts as
these may reasonably be held to sustain the popular creed as to there being bad fats
and good fats, and they teach us the lesson that in man, as in animals, there may be
a difference in the value of the fats we acquire, according as they are gained by one
means or by another.

The recent researches of L. Langer have certainly shown that the fatty tissues
of man vary at different ages, in the proportion of the fatty acids they contain.

I have had occasion, of late years, to watch with interest the process of somewhat rapid but quite wholesome gain in flesh in persons subjected to the treatment which I shall by and by describe. Most of these persons were treated by massage, and I have been accustomed to question the masseur or masseuse as to the manner in which the change takes place. Usually it is first seen in the face and neck, then it is noticed in the back and flanks, next in the belly, and finally in the limbs, the legs coming last in the order of gain, and sometimes remaining comparatively thin long after other parts have made remarkable and visible gain. These observations have been checked by careful measurements, so that I am sure of their correctness for people who fatten while at rest in bed. The order of increase might be different in people who fatten while afoot.

Facts of this nature suggest that the putting on of fat must be due to very generalized conditions, and be less under the control of local causes than is the nutrition of muscles, for, while it is true that in wasting from nerve-lesions the muscular and fatty tissues alike lessen, it is possible to cause by exercise rapid increase in the bulk of muscle in a limb or a part of a limb, but not in any way to cause direct and limited local increment of fat.

Looking back over the whole subject, it will be well for the physician to remember that increase of fat, to be a wholesome condition, should be accompanied by gain in quantity and quality of blood, and that while increase of flesh after illness is desirable, and a good test of successful recovery, it should always go along with improvement in color. Obesity with thin blood is one of the most unmanageable conditions I know of.

The exact relations of fatty tissue to the states of health are not as yet well understood; but, since on great exertion or prolonged mental or moral strain or in low fevers we lose fat rapidly, it may be taken for granted that each individual should possess a certain surplus of this readily-lost material. It is the one portion of our body which comes and goes in large amount. Even thin people have it in some quantity always ready, and, despite the fluctuations, every one has a standard share, which varies at different times of life. The mechanism which limits the storing away of an excess is almost unknown, and we are only aware that some foods and lack of exertion favor growth in fat, while action and lessened diet diminish it; but also we know that while any one can be made to lose weight, there are some persons who cannot be made to gain a pound by any possible device, so that in this, as in other things, to spend is easier than to get; although it is clear that the very thin must certainly live, so to speak, from hand to mouth, and have little for emergencies. Whether fat people possess greater power of resistance as against the fatal wasting of certain maladies or not, does not seem to be known, and I fancy that the popular medical belief is rather opposed to a belief in the vital endurance of those who are unusually fat.

That I am not pushing too far this idea of the indicative value of gain of weight may be further seen in persons who suffer from some incurable chronic malady, but who are in other respects well. The relief from their disease, even if temporary, is apt to be signalled by abrupt gain in weight. A remarkable illustration is to be found in those who suffer periodically from severe pain. Cessation of these attacks for a time is sure to result in the putting on of flesh. The case of Captain Catlin[10] is a good example. Owing to an accident of war, he lost a leg, and ever since has had severe neuralgic pain referred to the lost leg. These attacks depend almost altogether on storms. In years of fewest storms they are least numerous, and the bodily weight, which is never insufficient, rises. With their increase it lowers to a certain amount, beneath which it does not fall. His weight is, therefore, indirectly dependent upon the number of storms to the influence of which he is exposed.

At present, however, we have to do most largely with the means of attaining that moderate share of stored-away fat which seems to indicate a state of nutritive prosperity and to be essential to those physical needs, such as protection and padding, which fat subserves, no less than to its aesthetic value, as rounding the curves of the human form.

The study of the amount of the different forms of diet which is needed by people at rest, and by those who are active, is valuable only to enable us to construct dietaries with care for masses of men and where economy is an object. In dealing with cases such as I shall describe, it is needful usually to give and to have digested a surplus of food, so that we are more concerned now to know the forms of food which thin or fatten, and the means which aid us to digest temporarily an excess.

As to quantity, it suffices to say that while by lessening food we may easily and surely make people lose weight, we cannot be sure to fatten by merely increasing the amount of food given; something more is wanted in the way of digestives or tonics to enable the patient to prepare and appropriate what is given, and but too often we fail miserably in all our means of giving capacity to assimilate food. As I have said before, and wish to repeat, to gain in fat is, in the feeble, nearly always to gain in blood; and I hope to point out in these pages some of the means by which these ends can be attained.

.--The statements made on page 21 and the following paragraphs about obesity in England and with us are no longer exact, but have been allowed to stand in the text as recording facts true at the time of writing them, in 1877. At the present a medical observer familiar with both countries must several decided changes: more fat people, more people even enormously stout, are seen with us than formerly, and fewer of the "inordinately fat middle-aged people" in England than used to be encountered. With us the over-fat are chiefly to be found among the women of the well-to-do classes of the cities, and from thirty years old onward. They persecute the medical men to reduce their weight, and the vast number of advertisements of quack and proprietary remedies against obesity indicate how wide-spread the tendency must be.

Among women somewhat younger, as indeed among men, the American observer whose recollection takes him back twenty-five years must a more hopeful change, a very decided average increase of stature, not merely in height but in general development. This change is to be seen throughout the whole country, and must be taken first as a sign of improved conditions of food and manner of life, and next, if not more largely, of the new interest and partnership of girls in the wholesome activities of field and wood.

CHAPTER III.
ON THE SELECTION OF CASES FOR TREATMENT.

The remarks of the last chapter have, of course, wide and general application in disease, and naturally lead up to what I have to say as to the employment of the systematic treatment to describe which is my chief desire. Its use, as a whole, is limited to certain groups of cases. In some of the worst of them nothing else has succeeded hitherto, or at least as frequently. In others the need for its application must depend on convenience and the fact that all other and readier means have failed. It is, of course, difficult to state now all the groups of diseases in which it may be of value, for already physicians have begun to find it serviceable in some to which I had not thought of applying it,[11] and its sphere of usefulness is therefore likely to extend beyond the limits originally set by me. It will be well here, however, to state the various disorders in which it has seemed to me applicable. As regards some of them, I shall try briefly to indicate why their peculiarities point it out as needful.

There are, of course, numerous cases in which it becomes desirable to fatten and to make blood. In many of them these are easy tasks, and in some altogether hopeless. Persons who are recovering healthfully from fevers, pneumonias, and other temporary maladies gather flesh and make blood readily, and we need only to help them by the ordinary tonics, careful feeding, and change of air in due season.

It may not, however, be out of place to say here that when the convalescence from these maladies seems to be slower than is common, and ordinary tonics inefficient, massage and the use of electricity are not unimportant aids towards health, but in such cases require to be handled with an amount of caution which is less requisite in more chronic conditions of disordered health.

In other and fatal or graver maladies, such as, for example, advanced pulmonary phthisis, however proper it may be to fatten, it is almost an impossible task, and, as Pollock remarks, the lung-trouble may be advancing even while the patient is gaining in weight. Nevertheless, the earlier stages of pulmonary tuberculosis are suitable cases, and with sufficient attention to purity and frequent change of air in their rooms tubercular sufferers may be brought by this means to a point of improvement where open-air and altitude cures will have their best effects.

There remains a class of cases desirable to fatten and redden,--cases which are often, or usually, chronic in character, and present among them some of the most difficult problems which perplex the physician. If I pause to dwell upon these, it is because they exemplify forms of disease in which my method of treatment has had the largest success; it is because some of them are simply living records of the failure of every other rational plan and of many irrational ones; it is because many of them find no place in the text-book, however sadly familiar they are to the physician.

The group I would speak of contains that large number of people who are kept meagre and often also anaemic by constant dyspepsia, in its varied forms, or by those defects in assimilative processes which, while more obscure, are as fertile parents of similar mischiefs. Let us add the long-continued malarial poisonings, and we have a group of varied origin which is a moderate percentage of cases in which loss of weight and loss of color are noticeable, and in which the usual therapeutic methods do sometimes utterly fail.

For many of these, fresh air, exercise, change of scene, tonics, and stimulants are alike valueless; and for them the combined employment of the tonic influences I shall describe, when used with absolute rest, massage, and electricity, is often of inestimable service.

A portion of the class last referred to is one I have hinted at as the despair of the physician. It includes that large group of women, especially, said to have nervous exhaustion, or who are defined as having spinal irritation, if that be the prominent symptom. To it I must add cases in which, besides the wasting and anaemia, emotional manifestations predominate, and which are then called hysterical, whether or not they exhibit ovarian or uterine disorders.

Nothing is more common in practice than to see a young woman who falls below the health-standard, loses color and plumpness, is tired all the time, by and by has a tender spine, and soon or late enacts the whole varied drama of hysteria. As one or other set of symptoms is prominent she gets the appropriate label, and sometimes she continues to exhibit only the single phase of nervous exhaustion or of spinal irritation. Far more often she runs the gauntlet of nerve-doctors, gynaecologists, plaster jackets, braces, water-treatment, and all the fantastic variety of other cures.

It will be worth while to linger here a little and more sharply delineate the classes of cases I have just named.

I see every week--almost every day--women who when asked what is the matter reply, "Oh, I have nervous exhaustion." When further questioned, they answer that everything tires them. Now, it is vain to speak of all of these cases as hysterical, or as merely mimetic. It is quite sure that in the graver examples exercise quickens the pulse curiously, the tire shows in the face, or sometimes diarrhoea or nausea follows exertion, and though while under excitement or in the presence of some dominant motive they can do a good deal, the exhaustion which ensues is out of proportion to the exercise used.

I have rarely seen such a case which was not more or less lacking in color and which had not lost flesh; the exceptions being those troublesome instances of fat anaemic people which I shall by and by speak of more fully.

Perhaps a sketch of one of these cases will be better than any list of symptoms. A woman, most often between twenty and thirty years of age, undergoes a season of trial or encounters some prolonged strain. She may have undertaken the hard task of nursing a relative, and have gone through this severe duty with the addition of emotional excitement, swayed by hopes and fears, and forgetful of self and of what every one needs in the way of air and food and change when attempting this most trying task. In another set of cases an illness is the cause, and she never rallies entirely, or else some local uterine trouble starts the mischief, and, although this is cured, the doctor wonders that his patient does not get fat and ruddy again.

But, no matter how it comes about, whether from illness, anxiety, or prolonged physical effort, the woman grows pale and thin, eats little, or if she eats does not profit by it. Everything wearies her,--to sew, to write, to read, to walk,--and by and by the sofa or the bed is her only comfort. Every effort is paid for dearly, and she describes herself as aching and sore, as sleeping ill and awaking unrefreshed, and as needing constant stimulus and endless tonics. Then comes the mischievous role of bromides, opium, chloral, and brandy. If the case did not begin with uterine troubles, they soon appear, and are usually treated in vain if the general means employed to build up the bodily health fail, as in many of these cases they do fail. The same remark applies to the dyspepsias and constipation which further annoy the patient and embarrass the treatment. If such a person is by nature emotional she is sure to become more so, for even the firmest women lose self-control at last under incessant feebleness. Nor is this less true of men; and I have many a time seen soldiers who had ridden boldly with Sheridan or fought gallantly with Grant become, under the influence of painful nerve-wounds, as irritable and hysterically emotional as the veriest girl. If no rescue comes, the fate of women thus disordered is at last the bed. They acquire tender spines, and furnish the most lamentable examples of all the strange phenomena of hysteria.

The moral degradation which such cases undergo is pitiable. I have heard a good deal of the disciplinary usefulness of sickness, and this may well apply to brief and grave, and what I might call wholesome, maladies. Undoubtedly I have seen a few people who were ennobled by long sickness, but far more often the result is to cultivate self-love and selfishness and to take away by slow degrees the healthful mastery which all human beings should retain over their own emotions and wants.

There is one fatal addition to the weight which tends to destroy women who suffer in the way I have described. It is the self-sacrificing love and over-careful sympathy of a mother, a sister, or some other devoted relative. Nothing is more curious, nothing more sad and pitiful, than these partnerships between the sick and selfish and the sound and over-loving. By slow but sure degrees the healthy life is absorbed by the sick life, in a manner more or less injurious to both, until, sometimes too late for remedy, the growth of the evil is seen by others. Usually the individual withdrawn from wholesome duties to minister to the caprices of hysterical sensitiveness is the person of a household who feels most for the invalid, and who for this very reason suffers the most. The patient has pain,--a tender spine, for example; she is urged to give it rest. She cannot read; the self-constituted nurse reads to her. At last light hurts her eyes; the mother or sister remains shut up with her all day in a darkened room. A draught of air is supposed to do harm, and the doors and windows are closed, and the ingenuity of kindness is taxed to imagine new sources of like trouble, until at last, as I have seen more than once, the window-cracks are stuffed with cotton, the chimney is stopped, and even the keyhole guarded. It is easy to see where this all leads to: the nurse falls ill, and a new victim is found. I have seen an hysterical, anaemic girl kill in this way three generations of nurses. If you tell the patient she is basely selfish, she is probably amazed, and wonders at your cruelty. To cure such a case you must morally alter as well as physically amend, and nothing less will answer. The first step needful is to break up the companionship, and to substitute the firm kindness of a well-trained hired nurse.[12]

Another form of evil to be encountered in these cases is less easy to deal with. Such an invalid has by unhappy chance to live with some near relative whose temperament is also nervous and who is impatient or irritable. Two such people produce endless mischief for each other. Occasionally there is a strange incompatibility which it is difficult to define. The two people who, owing to their relationship, depend the one on the other, are, for no good reason, made unhappy by their several peculiarities. Lifelong annoyance results, and for them there is no divorce possible.

In a smaller number of cases, which have less tendency to emotional disturbances, the phenomena are more simple. You have to deal with a woman who has lost flesh and grown colorless, but has no hysterical tendencies. She is merely a person hopelessly below the standard of health and subject to a host of aches and pains, without notable organic disease. Why such people should sometimes be so hard to cure I cannot say. But the sad fact remains. Iron, acids, travel, water-cures, have for a certain proportion of them no value, or little value, and they remain for years feeble and forever tired. For them, as for the whole class, the pleasures of life are limited by this perpetual weariness and by the asthenopia which they rarely escape, and which, by preventing them from reading, leaves them free to study day after day their accumulating aches and distresses.

Medical opinion must, of course, vary as to the causes which give rise to the familiar disorders I have so briefly sketched, but I imagine that few physicians placed face to face with such cases would not feel sure that if they could insure to these patients a liberal gain in fat and in blood they would be certain to need very little else, and that the troubles of stomach, bowels, and uterus would speedily vanish.

I need hardly say that I do not mean by this that the mere addition of blood and normal flesh is what we want, but that their gradual increase will be a visible result of the multitudinous changes in digestive, assimilative, and secretive power in which the whole economy inevitably shares, and of which my relation of cases will be a better statement than any more general one I could make here.

Such has certainly been the result of my own very ample experience. If I succeed in first altering the moral atmosphere which has been to the patient like the very breathing of evil, and if I can add largely to the weight and fill the vessels with red blood, I am usually sure of giving general relief to a host of aches, pains, and varied disabilities. If I fail, it is because I fail in these very points, or else because I have overlooked or undervalued some serious organic tissue-change. It must be said that now and then one is beaten by a patient who has an unconquerable taste for invalidism, or one to whom the change of moral atmosphere is not bracing, or by sheer laziness, as in the case of a lady who said to me, as a final argument, "Why should I walk when I can have a negro boy to push me in a chair?"

It will have been seen that I am careful in the selection of cases for this treatment. Conducted under the best circumstances for success, it involves a good deal that is costly. Neither does it answer as well, and for obvious reasons, in hospital wards; and this is most true in regard to persons who are demonstratively hysterical. As a rule, the worse the case, the more emaciated, the more easy is it to manage, to control, and to cure. It is, as Playfair remarks, the half-ill who constitute the difficult cases.

I am also very careful as to being sure of the absence of certain forms of organic disease before flattering myself with the probability of success. But not all organic troubles forbid the use of this treatment. Advanced Bright's disease does, though the early stages of contracted kidney are decidedly benefited by it, if proper diet be prescribed; but intestinal troubles which are not tubercular or malignant do not; nor do moderate signs of chronic pulmonary deposits, or bronchitis.[13]

Some special consideration needs to be given to the subject of heart-disease. Especially in cases of broken compensation, by lessening the work required of the heart so that it needs to beat both less often and with less force, the simple maintenance of the recumbent position is a great aid to recovery, and massage properly used will still further relieve the heart. Disturbed compensation is usually accompanied by failure of nutrition, often by distinct anaemia, and these and the anxiety which naturally enough affects the mind of a person with cardiac disorder are all best handled, at first at least, by quiet and rest. Later, the methods of Schott, baths and resistance movements, may carry the improvement further. Even in old and established cases of valvular disease much may be done if the patient have confidence and the physician courage enough to insist upon a sufficient length of rest. The palpitation and dyspnoea of exophthalmic goitre are promptly helped by rest and massage, and with other suitable measures added, cures may be effected even in this intractable ailment.

In former editions I have advised against any attempt to treat the true melancholias, which are not mere depression of spirits from loss of all hope of relief, by this method, but wider experience has convinced me that rest and seclusion may often be successfully prescribed to a certain extent and in certain cases.

Those in which the most good has been done have been the cases of agitated melancholia with attacks, more or less clearly periodic, of excitement, during which their delusions take acuter hold of them and drive them to wild extravagance of noisy talk and bodily restlessness. Whether such patients must be put to bed or not one must judge in each instance, taking into account the general nutrition. In my own practice I certainly do put them to bed now much oftener than formerly. It is not desirable to keep them there for the six or eight weeks which full treatment would demand. Usually it will be of advantage to order, say, two weeks of "absolute rest," observing the usual precautions about getting the patient up, prescribing bed again when the early signs of an attack of agitation appear, and keeping him there for a couple of days on each occasion, during which the full schedule of treatment is to be minutely carried out.

Goodell and, more recently, Playfair have pointed out the fact that some cases of disease of the uterine appendages such as would ordinarily be considered hopeless, except for surgical treatment, have in their hands recovered to all appearances entirely; and my own list of patients condemned to the removal of the ovaries but recovering and remaining well has now grown to a formidable length. Playfair observes also that he believes it possible that in even very severe and extensive disease the health of the patient may be sufficiently improved to render operation unnecessary.[14]

In cases of floating kidney some very satisfactory results have been reached by long rest; and although it may be necessary to keep the patient supine for three months or more, the reasonable probability of permanent replacement of the organ is much greater than from operative attempts at fixation, apart from the danger and pain of surgical procedures. Persons with floating kidney are nearly always thin, often giving a history of rapid loss of weight, have usually various symptoms of gastric and intestinal disturbance, and present therefore subjects in all ways suitable for a fattening and blood-making *regime* which shall furnish padding to hold the kidney firmly in its normal place.

The treatment of locomotor ataxia and some allied states by this method, with certain modifications, has yielded such good results that I now undertake with reasonable confidence the charge of such patients; and the subject is so important and has as yet influenced so little the futile drugging treatment of these wretched cases that it seems worth while to devote a special chapter to it, although the affections named can scarcely be said to be included under the head of neurasthenic disease.

In the following chapters I shall treat of the means which I have employed, and shall not hesitate to give such minute details as shall enable others to profit by my failures and successes. In describing the remedies used, and the mode of using them in combination, I shall relate a sufficient number of cases to illustrate both the happier results and the causes of occasional failure.

The treatment I am about to describe consists in seclusion, certain forms of diet, rest in bed, massage (or manipulation), and electricity; and I desire to insist anew on the fact that in most cases it is the combined use of these means that is wanted. How far they may be modified or used separately in some instances, I shall have occasion to point out as I discuss the various agencies alluded to.

CHAPTER IV.
SECLUSION.

It is rare to find any of the class of patients I have described so free from the influence of their habitual surroundings as to make it easy to treat them in their own homes. It is needful to disentangle them from the meshes of old habits and to remove them from contact with those who have been the willing slaves of their caprices. I have often made the effort to treat them where they have lived and to isolate them there, but I have rarely done so without promising myself that I would not again complicate my treatment by any such embarrassments. Once separate the patient from the moral and physical surroundings which have become part of her life of sickness, and you will have made a change which will be in itself beneficial and will enormously aid in the treatment which is to follow. Of course this step is not essential in such cases as are merely anaemic, feeble, and thin, owing to distinct causes, like the exhaustion of overwork, blood-losses, dyspepsia, low fevers, or nursing. There are but too many women who have broken down under such causes and failed to climb again to the level of health, despite all that could be done for them; and when such persons are free from emotional excitement or hysterical complications there is no reason why the seclusion needful to secure them repose of mind should not be pleasantly modified in accordance with the dictates of common sense. Very often a little experimentation as to what they will profitably bear in the way of visits and the like will inform us, as their treatment progresses, how far such indulgence is of use or free from hurtful influences. Cases of extreme neurasthenia in men accompanied with nutritive failures require as to this matter cautious handling, because, for some reason, the ennui of rest and seclusion is far better borne by women than by the other sex.

Even in cases whose moral aspects do not at once suggest an imperative need for seclusion it is well to remember, as regards neurasthenic people, that the treatment involves for a time daily visits of some length from the masseur, the doctor, and possibly an electrician, and that to add to these even a single friendly visitor is often too much to be readily borne; but I am now speaking chiefly of the large and troublesome class of thin-blooded emotional women, for whom a state of weak health has become a long and, almost I might say, a cherished habit. For them there is often no success possible until we have broken up the whole daily drama of the sick-room, with its little selfishness and its craving for sympathy and indulgence. Nor should we hesitate to insist upon this change, for not only shall we then act in the true interests of the patient, but we shall also confer on those near to her an inestimable benefit. An hysterical girl is, as Wendell Holmes has said in his decisive phrase, a vampire who sucks the blood of the healthy people about her; and I may add that pretty surely where there is one hysterical girl there will be soon or late two sick women. If circumstances oblige us to treat such a person in her own home, let us at least change her room, and also have it well understood how far we are to control her surroundings and to govern as to visitors and the company of her own family. Do as we may, we shall always lessen thus our chances of success, but we shall certainly not altogether destroy them.

I should add here a few words of caution as to the time of year best fitted for treatment. In the summer seclusion is often undesirable when the patient is well enough to gain help by change of air; moreover, at this season massage is less agreeable than in winter, and, as a rule, I find it harder to feed and to fatten persons at rest during our summer heats. That this rule is not without exception has been shown by Drs. Goodell and Sinkler, both of whom have attained some remarkable successes in midsummer.

One of the questions of most importance in the carrying out of this treatment is the choice of a nurse. Just as it is desirable to change the home of the patient, her diet, her atmosphere, so also is it well, for the mere alterative value of such change, to surround her with strangers and to put aside any nurse with whom she may have grown familiar. As I have sometimes succeeded in treating invalids in their own homes, so have I occasionally been able to carry through cases nursed by a mother, or sister, or friend of exceptional firmness; but to attempt this is to be heavily handicapped, and the position should never be accepted if it be possible to make other arrangements. Any firm, intelligent woman of tact, a stranger to the patient, is better than the old style of nurse, now, happily, disappearing. The nurse for these cases ought to be a young, active, quick-witted woman, capable of firmly but gently controlling her patient. She ought to be intelligent, able to interest her patient, to read aloud, and to write letters. The more of these cases she has seen and nursed, the easier becomes the task of the doctor. Young, I have said she ought to be, but youthful would be a better word. If, as she grows older, the nurse loses the strenuous enthusiasm with which she made her first entrance into her work, scarcely any amount of conscientious devotion or experience will ever replace it; but there are fortunate people who seem never to grow old in this sense. It is always to be borne in mind that most of these patients are over-sensitive, refined, and educated women, for whom the clumsiness, or want of neatness, or bad manners, or immodesty of a nurse may be a sore and steadily-increasing trial. To be more or less isolated for two months in a room, with one constant attendant, however good, is hard enough for any one to endure; and certain quite small faults or defects in a nurse may make her a serious impediment to the treatment, because no mere technical training will dispense in the nurse any more than in the physician with those finer natural qualifications which make their training available. Over-harshness is in some ways worse than over-easiness, because it makes less pleasant the relation between nurse and patient, and the latter should regard the former as her "next friend." Let the nurse, therefore, place upon the doctor the burden of decision in disputed matters; his position will not be injured with the patient by strict enforcement of the letter of the law, while the nurse's may be. But one nurse will suit one patient and not another: so that I never hesitate to change my nurse if she does not fit the case, and to change if necessary more than once.

The degree of seclusion should be prescribed from the first, and it is far better to find that the original rules may be profitably relaxed than to be obliged to draw the lines more strictly when the patient has at first been indulged. For instance, it is well to forbid the receipt of any letters from home, unless anxious relatives insist that the patient must have home news. In that case the letters should be mere bulletins, should contain nothing, no matter how trifling, that might annoy a too sensitive person, and, most important of all, should come to the nurse and by her be read to the patient.

CHAPTER V.
REST.

I have said more than once in the early chapters of this little volume that the treatment I wished to advise as of use in a certain range of cases was made up of rest, massage, electricity, and over-feeding. I said that the use of large amounts of food while at rest, more or less entire, was made possible by the practice of kneading the muscles and by moving them with currents able to effect this end. I desire now to discuss in turn the modes in which I employ rest, massage, and electricity, and, as I have promised, I shall take pains to give, in regard to these three subjects, the fullest details, because success in the treatment depends, I am sure, on the care with which we look after a number of things each in itself apparently of slight moment.

I have no doubt that many doctors have seen fit at times to put their patients at rest for great or small lengths of time, but the person who of all others within my knowledge used this means most, and used it so as to obtain the best results, was the late Professor Samuel Jackson. He was in the habit of making his patients remain in bed for many weeks at a time, and, if I recall his cases well, he used this treatment in just the class of disorders among women which have given me the best results. What these are I have been at some pains to define, and I have now only to show why in such people rest is of service, and what I mean by rest, and how I apply it.

In No. IV. of Dr. Seguin's series of American Clinical Lectures, I was at some pains to point out the value of repose in neuralgias, and especially sciatica, in myelitis, and in the early stages of locomotor ataxia, and I have since then had the pleasure of seeing these views very fully accepted. I shall now confine myself chiefly to its use in the various forms of weakness which exist with thin blood and wasting, with or without distinct lesions of the stomach, womb, or other organs.

Whether we shall ask a patient to walk or to take rest is a question which turns up for answer almost every day in practice. Most often we incline to insist on exercise, and are led to do so from a belief that many people walk too little, and that to move about a good deal every day is well for everybody. I think we are as often wrong as right. A good brisk daily walk is for well folks a tonic, breaks down old tissues, and creates a wholesome demand for food. The same is true for some sick people. The habit of horse-exercise or a long walk every day is needed to cure or to aid in the cure of disordered stomach and costive bowels, but if all exertion gives rise only to increase of trouble, to extreme sense of fatigue, to nausea, to headache, what shall we do? And suppose that tonics do not help to make exertion easy, and that the great tonic of change of air fails us, shall we still persist? And here lies the trouble: there are women who mimic fatigue, who indulge themselves in rest on the least pretence, who have no symptoms so truly honest that we need care to regard them. These are they who spoil their own nervous systems as they spoil their children, when they have them, by yielding to the least desire and teaching them to dwell on little pains. For such people there is no help but to insist on self-control and on daily use of the limbs. They must be told to exert themselves, and made to do so if that can be. If they are young, this is easy enough. If they have grown to middle life, and created habits of self-indulgence, the struggle is often useless. But few, however, among these women are free from some defect of blood or tissue, either original or acquired as a result of years of indolence and attention to aches and ailments which should never have had given to them more than a passing thought, and which certainly should not have been made an excuse for the sofa or the bed.

Sometimes the question is easy to settle. If you find a woman who is in good condition as to color and flesh, and who is always able to do what it pleases her to do, and who is tired by what does not please her, that is a woman to order out of bed and to control with a firm and steady will. That is a woman who is to be made to walk, with no regard to her complaints, and to be made to persist until exertion ceases to give rise to the mimicry of fatigue. In such cases the man who can insure belief in his opinions and obedience to his decrees secures very often most brilliant and sometimes easy success; and it is in such cases that women who are in all other ways capable doctors fail, because they do not obtain the needed control over those of their own sex. I have been struck with this a number of times, but I have also seen that to be too long and too habitually in the hands of one physician, even the wisest, is for some cases of hysteria the main difficulty in the way of a cure,--it is so easy to disobey the familiar friendly attendant, so hard to do this where the physician is a stranger. But we all know well enough the personal value of certain doctors for certain cases. Mere hygienic advice will win a victory in the hands of one man and obtain no good results in those of another, for we are, after all, artists who all use the same means to an end but fail or succeed according to our method of using them. There are still other cases in which mischievous tendencies to repose, to endless tire, to hysterical symptoms, and to emotional displays have grown out of defects of nutrition so distinct that no man ought to think for these persons of mere exertion as a sole means of cure. The time comes for that, but it should not come until entire rest has been used, with other means, to fit them for making use of their muscles. Nothing upsets these cases like over-exertion, and the attempt to make them walk usually ends in some mischievous emotional display, and in creating a new reason for thinking that they cannot walk. As to the two sets of cases just sketched, no one need hesitate; the one must walk, the other should not until we have bettered her nutritive state. She may be able to drag herself about, but no good will be done by making her do so. But between these two classes, and allied by certain symptoms to both, lie the larger number of such cases, giving us every kind of real and imagined symptom, and dreadfully well fitted to puzzle the most competent physician. As a rule, no harm is done by rest, even in such people as give us doubts about whether it is or is not well for them to exert themselves. There are plenty of these women who are just well enough to make it likely that if they had motive enough for exertion to cause them to forget themselves they would find it useful. In the doubt I am rather given to insisting on rest, but the rest I like for them is not at all their notion of rest. To lie abed half the day, and sew a little and read a little, and be interesting as invalids and excite sympathy, is all very well, but when they are bidden to stay in bed a month, and neither to read, write, nor sew, and to have one nurse, who is not a relative,--then repose becomes for some women a rather bitter medicine, and they are glad enough to accept the order to rise and go about when the doctor issues a mandate which has become pleasantly welcome and eagerly looked for. I do not think it easy to make a mistake in this matter unless the woman takes with morbid delight to the system of enforced rest, and unless the doctor is a person of feeble will. I have never met myself with any serious trouble about getting out of bed any woman for whom I thought rest needful, but it has happened to others, and the man who resolves to send any nervous woman to bed must be quite sure that she will obey him when the time comes for her to get up.

I have, of course, made use of every grade of rest for my patients, from repose on a lounge for some hours a day up to entire rest in bed. In milder forms of neurasthenic disease, in cases of slight general depression not properly to be called melancholias, in the lesser grades of pure brain-tire, or where this is combined with some physical debility, I often order a "modified" or "partial rest." A detailed schedule of the day is ordered for such patients, with as much minuteness of care as for those undergoing "full rest" in bed. Here the patient's or the household's usual hours may be consulted, a definite amount of time allotted to duties, business, and exercise, and certain hours left blank, to be filled, within limits, at the patient's discretion or that of the nurse.

So many nervous people are worried with indecision, with inability to make up their minds to the simplest actions, that to have the responsibility of choice taken away greatly lessens their burdens. It lessens, too, the burdens which may be placed upon them by outside action if they can refuse this or that because they are under orders as to hours.

The following is a skeleton form of such a schedule. The hours, the food, the occupations suggested in each one will vary according to the sex, age, position, desires, intelligence, and opportunities of the patient.

7.30 A.M. Cocoa, coffee, hot milk, beef-extract, or hot water. Bath (temperature stated). Rough rub with towel or flesh-brush: bathing and rubbing may be done by attendant. Lie down a few minutes after finishing.

8.30 A.M. Breakfast in bed. (Detail as to diet. Tonic, aperient, malt extract as ordered.) May read letters, paper, etc., if eyes are good.

10-11 A.M. Massage, if required, is usually ordered one hour after breakfast; or Swedish movements are given at that time. An hour's rest follows massage. Less rest is needed after the movements. (Milk or broth after massage.)

12 M. Rise and dress slowly. If gymnastics or massage are not ordered, may rise earlier. May see visitors, attend to household affairs, or walk out.

1.30 P.M. Luncheon. (Malt, tonic, etc., ordered.) In invalids this should be the chief meal of the day. Rest, lying down, not in bed, for an hour after.

3 P.M. Drive (use street-cars or walk) one to two and a half hours. (Milk or soup on return.)

7 P.M. Supper. (Malt, tonic, etc., ordered; detail of diet.)

Bed at 10 P.M. Hot milk or other food at bedtime.

This schedule is modified for convalescent patients after rest-treatment by orders as to use of the eyes: letter-writing is usually forbidden, walking distinctly directed or forbidden, as the case may require. It may be changed by putting the exercise, massage, or gymnastics in the afternoon, for example, and leaving the morning, as soon as the rest after breakfast is finished, for business. Men needing partial rest may thus find time to attend to their affairs.

If massage is not ordered, there is nothing in this routine which costs money, and I have found it apply usefully in the case of hospital and dispensary patients.

In carrying out my general plan of treatment in extreme cases it is my habit to ask the patient to remain in bed from six weeks to two months. At first, and in some cases for four or five weeks, I do not permit the patient to sit up, or to sew or write or read, or to use the hands in any active way except to clean the teeth. Where at first the most absolute rest is desirable, as in cases of heart-disease, or where there is a floating kidney, I arrange to have the bowels and water passed while lying down, and the patient is lifted on to a lounge for an hour in the morning and again at bedtime, and then lifted back again into the newly-made bed. In most cases of weakness, treated by rest, I insist on the patient being fed by the nurse, and, when well enough to sit up in bed, I order that the meats shall be cut up, so as to make it easier for the patient to feed herself.

In many cases I allow the patient to sit up in order to obey the calls of nature, but I am always careful to have the bowels kept reasonably free from costiveness, knowing well how such a state and the efforts it gives rise to enfeeble a sick person.

The daily sponging bath is to be given by the nurse, and should be rapidly and skilfully done. It may follow the first food of the day, the early milk, or cocoa, or coffee, or, if preferred, may be used before noon, or at bedtime, which is found in some cases to be best and to promote sleep.

For some reason, the act of bathing, or even the being bathed, is mysteriously fatiguing to certain invalids, and if so I have the general sponging done for a time but thrice a week.

Most of these patients suffer from use of the eyes, and this makes it needful to prohibit reading and writing, and to have all correspondence carried on through the nurse. But many neurasthenic people also suffer from being read to, or, in other words, from any prolonged effort at attention. In these cases it will be found that if the nurse will read the morning paper, and as she does so relate such news as may be of interest, the patient will bear it very well, and will by degrees come to endure the hearing of such reading as is already more or less familiar.

Usually, after a fortnight I permit the patient to be read to,--one to three hours a day,--but I am daily amazed to see how kindly nervous and anaemic women take to this absolute rest, and how little they complain of its monotony. In fact, the use of massage and the battery, with the frequent comings of the nurse with food, and the doctor's visits, seem so to fill up the day as to make the treatment less tiresome than might be supposed. And, besides this, the sense of comfort which is apt to come about the fifth or sixth day,--the feeling of ease, and the ready capacity to digest food, and the growing hope of final cure, fed as it is by present relief,--all conspire to make most patients contented and tractable.

The intelligent and watchful physician must, of course, know how far to enforce and when to relax these rules. When it is needful, as it sometimes is, to prolong the state of rest to two or three months, the patient may need at the close occupation of some kind, and especially such as, while it does not tax the eyes, gives the hands something to do, the patient being, we suppose, by this time able to sit up in bed during a part of the day.

The moral uses of enforced rest are readily estimated. From a restless life of irregular hours, and probably endless drugging, from hurtful sympathy and over-zealous care, the patient passes to an atmosphere of quiet, to order and control, to the system and care of a thorough nurse, to an absence of drugs, and to simple diet. The result is always at first, whatever it may be afterwards, a sense of relief, and a remarkable and often a quite abrupt disappearance of many of the nervous symptoms with which we are all of us only too sadly familiar.

All the moral uses of rest and isolation and change of habits are not obtained by merely insisting on the physical conditions needed to effect these ends. If the physician has the force of character required to secure the confidence and respect of his patients, he has also much more in his power, and should have the tact to seize the proper occasions to direct the thoughts of his patients to the lapse from duties to others, and to the selfishness which a life of invalidism is apt to bring about. Such moral medication belongs to the higher sphere of the doctor's duties, and, if he means to cure his patient permanently, he cannot afford to neglect them. Above all, let him be careful that the masseuse and the nurse do not talk of the patient's ills, and let him by degrees teach the sick person how very essential it is to speak of her aches and pains to no one but himself.

I have often asked myself why rest is of value in the cases of which I am now speaking, and I have already alluded briefly to some of the modes in which it is of use.

Let us take first the simpler cases. We meet now and then with feeble people who are dyspeptic, and who find that exercise after a meal, or indeed much exercise on any day, is sure to cause loss of power or lessened power to digest food. The same thing is seen in an extreme degree in the well-known experiment of causing a dog to run violently after eating, in which case digestion is entirely suspended. Whether these results be due to the calling off of blood from the gastric organs to the muscles, or whether the nervous system is, for some reason, unable to evolve at the same time the force needed for a double purpose, is not quite clear, but the fact is undoubted, and finds added illustrations in many of the class of exhausted women. It is plain that this trouble exists in some of them. It is likely that it is present in a larger number. The use of rest in these people admits of no question. If we are to give them the means in blood and flesh of carrying on the work of life, it must be done with the aid of the stomach, and we must humor that organ until it is able to act in a more healthy manner under ordinary conditions. It may be wise to add that occasional cases of nervousness or of nervous disturbance of digestion are seen in which the patient assimilates food better if permitted to move about directly after a meal; and I recall one instance of very persistent gastric catarrh where the uncomfortable symptoms following meals only began to disappear when as an experiment the patient was ordered to take a quiet half-hour's stroll after each meal, instead of the rest usually ordered.

I am often asked how I can expect by such a system to rest the organs of mind.

No act of will can force them to be at rest. To this I should answer that it is not the mere half-automatic intellectuation which is harmful in men or women subject to states of feebleness or neurasthenia, and that the systematic vigorous use of mind on distinct problems is within some form of control. It is thought with the friction of worry which injures, and unless we can secure an absence of this, it is vain to hope for help by the method I am describing. The man harassed by business anxieties, the woman with morbidly-developed or ungoverned maternal instincts, will only illustrate the causes of failure. Perhaps in all dubious cases Dr. Playfair's rule is not a bad one, to consider, and to let the patient consider, this mode of treatment as a hopeful experiment, which may have to be abandoned, and which is valueless without the cordial and submissive assistance of the patient.

The muscular system in many of such patients--I mean in ever-weary, thin and thin-blooded persons--is doing its work with constant difficulty. As a result, fatigue comes early, is extreme, and lasts long. The demand for nutritive aid is ahead of the supply, or else the supply is incompetent as to quality, and before the tissues are rebuilded a new demand is made, so that the materials of disintegration accumulate, and do this the more easily because the eliminative organs share in the general defects. And these are some of the reasons why anaemic people are always tired; but, besides this, all real sensations are magnified by women whose nervous systems have become sensitive owing to a life of attention to their ailments, and so at last it becomes hard to separate the true from the false, and we are thus led to be too sceptical as to the presence of real causes of annoyance. Certain it is that rest, under proper conditions, is found by such sufferers to be a great relief; but rest alone will not answer, and it is needful, as I shall show, to bring to our help certain other means, in order to secure all the good which repose may be made to insure.

In dealing with this, as with every other medical means, it is well to recall that in our attempts to help we may sometimes do harm, and we must make sure that in causing the largest share of good we do the least possible evil.

"The one goes with the other, as shadow with light, and to no therapeutic measure does this apply more surely than to the use of rest.

"Let us take the simplest case,--that which arises daily in the treatment of joint-troubles or broken bones. We put the limb in splints, and thus, for a time, check its power to move. The bone knits, or the joint gets well; but the muscles waste, the skin dries, the nails may for a time cease to grow, nutrition is brought down, as an arithmetician would say, to its lowest terms, and when the bone or joint is well we have a limb which is in a state of disease. As concerns broken bones, the evil may be slight and easy of relief, if the surgeon will but remember that when joints are put at rest too long they soon fall a prey to a form of arthritis, which is the more apt to be severe the older the patient is, and may be easily avoided by frequent motion of the joints, which, to be healthful, exact a certain share of daily movement. If, indeed, with perfect stillness of the fragments we could have the full life of a limb in action, I suspect that the cure of the break might be far more rapid.

"What is true of the part is true of the whole. When we put the entire body at rest we create certain evils while doing some share of good, and it is therefore our part to use such means as shall, in every case, lessen and limit the ills we cannot wholly avoid. How to reach these ends I shall by and by state, but for a brief space I should like to dwell on some of the bad results which come of our efforts to reach through rest in bed all the good which it can give us, and to these points I ask the most thoughtful attention, because upon the care with which we meet and provide for them depends the value which we will get out of this most potent means of treatment.

"When we put patients in bed and forbid them to rise or to make use of their muscles, we at once lessen appetite, weaken digestion in many cases, constipate the bowels, and enfeeble circulation."[15]

When we put the muscles at absolute rest we create certain difficulties, because the normal acts of repeated movement insure a certain rate of nutrition which brings blood to the active parts, and without which the currents flow more largely around than through the muscles. The lessened blood-supply is a result of diminished functional movement, and we need to create a constant demand in the inactive parts. But, besides this, every active muscle is practically a throbbing heart, squeezing its vessels empty while in motion, and relaxing, so as to allow them to fill up anew. Thus, both for itself and in its relations to the areolar spaces and to the rest of the body, its activity is functionally of service. Then, also, the vessels, unaided by changes of posture and by motion, lose tone, and the distant local circuits, for all of these reasons, cease to receive their normal supply, so that defects of nutrition occur, and, with these, defects of temperature.

"I was struck with the extent to which these evils may go, in the case of Mrs. P., aet. 52, who was brought to me from New Jersey, having been in bed fifteen years. I soon knew that she was free of grave disease, and had stayed in bed at first because there was some lack of power and much pain on rising, and at last because she had the firm belief that she could not walk. After a week's massage I made her get up. I had won her full trust, and she obeyed, or tried to obey me, like a child. But she would faint and grow deadly pale, even if seated a short time. The heart-beats rose from sixty to one hundred and thirty, and grew feeble; the breath came fast, and she had to lie down at once. Her skin was dry, sallow, and bloodless, her muscles flabby; and when, at last, after a fortnight more, I set her on her feet again, she had to endure for a time the most dreadful vertigo and alarming palpitations of the heart, while her feet, in a few minutes of feeble walking, would swell so as to present the most strange appearance. By and by all this went away, and in a month she could walk, sit up, sew, read, and, in a word, live like others. She went home a well-cured woman.

"Let us think, then, when we put a person in bed, that we are lessening the heart-beats some twenty a minute, nearly a third; that we are causing the tardy blood to linger in the by-ways of the blood-round, for it has its by-ways; that rest in bed binds the bowels, and tends to destroy the desire to eat; and that muscles at rest too long get to be unhealthy and shrunken in substance. Bear these ills in mind, and be ready to meet them, and we shall have answered the hard question of how to help by rest without hurt to the patient."

When I first made use of this treatment I allowed my patients to get up too suddenly, and in some cases I thus brought on relapses and a return of the feeling of painful fatigue. I also saw in some of these cases what I still see at times under like circumstances,--a rapid loss of flesh.

I now begin by permitting the patient to sit up in bed, then to feed herself, and next to sit up out of bed a few minutes at bedtime. In a week, she is desired to sit up fifteen minutes twice a day, and this is gradually increased until, at the end of six to twelve weeks, she rests on the bed only three to five hours daily. Even after she moves about and goes out, I insist for two months on absolute repose at least two or three hours daily, and this must be understood to mean seclusion as well as bodily quiet, free from the intrusion of household cares, visitors, or any form of emotion or excitement, pleasureable or otherwise. In cases of long-standing it may be desirable to continue this period of isolation and to order as well an hour's lying down after each meal for many months, in some such methodical way as is suggested in the schedule on page 64.

The use of a hammock is found by some people to be a very agreeable change from the bed during a part of the day.

The physician who discharges his patient when she rises from her bed after her two or three months' treatment, or who neglects to consider the moral and mental needs and aspects of each case, will find that many will relapse. Even when the patient has left the direct care of the doctor and returned to home and its avocations she will find help and comfort in the knowledge that she can apply to him if necessary, and it is well to hold some sort of relation by occasional visits or correspondence, however brief, for six months or a year after treatment has been completed.

CHAPTER VI.
MASSAGE.

How to deprive rest of its evils is the title with which I might very well have labelled this chapter. I have pointed out what I mean by rest, how it hurts, and how it seems to help; and, as I believe that it is useful in most cases only if employed in conjunction with other means, the study of these becomes of the first importance.

The two aids which by degrees I learned to call upon with confidence to enable me to use rest without doing harm are massage and electricity. We have first to deal with massage, and I give some care to the description of details, because even now it is imperfectly understood in this country, and because I wish to emphasize some facts about it which are not well known, I think, on either side of the Atlantic.

Massage in some form has long been in use in the East, and is well known as the *lommi-lommi* of the slothful inhabitants of the Sandwich Islands. In Japan it is reserved as an occupation for the blind, whose delicate sense of feeling might, I should think, very well fit them for this task. It is, however, in these countries less used in disease than as the luxury of the rich; nor can I find in the few books on the subject that it has been resorted to habitually as a tonic in Europe, or otherwise than as a means of treating local disorders.

It is many years since I first saw in this city general massage used by a charlatan in a case of progressive paralysis. The temporary results he obtained were so remarkable that I began soon after to employ it in locomotor ataxia, in which it sometimes proved of signal value, and in other forms of spinal and local disease. At first I had to train nurses to use it, but I soon found that, although it was of some service to their patients, no one could use massage well who was not continually engaged in doing it. Some men do it better than any woman; but I prefer, nevertheless, for obvious reasons, to reserve men for male patients, except that in cases where *strength* is of moment, as in the forced movements and the very hard rubbing needed for old articular adhesions, in which force must be exercised without violence, it is usually impossible to secure the necessary power in a feminine manipulator.

A few years later I resorted to it in the first cases which I treated by rest, and I very soon found that I had in it an agent little understood and of singular utility.

It will be necessary, in pursuance of my plan, to describe as minutely as the limits of a chapter will allow how and why this means is employed. The process and order of what is known to the manipulator as "general massage" follows.

After three or four days in bed have somewhat accustomed the patient to the general routine of treatment, a masseur or masseuse is set to work. If any special care is needed,--the avoidance of manipulating one part or added attention to another, tender handling of a sensitive or timid patient,--these matters have been ordered in advance by the physician. An hour midway between meals is chosen, and, the patient lying in bed between blankets, the manipulator begins, usually with the feet. A few rapid rubs of the whole foot and leg are given to start with; then the leg, except the foot and ankle, is covered up, and the operation commences upon the foot, of which the skin is picked up and rolled between the fingers, the whole foot receiving careful attention,--the toes are pulled, bent, and moved in every direction, the inter-osseous groups worked over with the thumbs and fingers or finger-tips, the larger muscles and subcutaneous tissues squeezed and kneaded, and last the whole mass of the foot rolled and pressed against the bones with both hands. A few rapid upward strokings with some force complete the treatment of the part, and the ankle is next dealt with. The joint is moved in every possible direction, slowly but firmly, the crevices between the articulating bones sought out and kneaded with the finger-tips, and the foot and ankle are then carefully covered. After the same rapid stroking upward of the leg with which it began has been repeated for the sake of the slight stimulation of the skin-vessels and nerves, the muscles of the leg are treated, first by friction of the more superficially placed masses, then by careful deep kneading (*petrissage*) of the large muscles of the calf, twisting, pressing, and rolling them about the bone with one hand while the other supports the limb. In fat or heavily-muscled subjects it may be necessary to use both hands to get sufficient grasp of the muscles. The tibialis anticus and muscles of the outer side of the leg are operated upon by rolling them under the finger-tips and by pressing with the thumb while firmly pushing upward from the ankle to the knee. At brief intervals the manipulator seizes the limb in both hands and lightly runs the grasp upward, so as to favor the flow of the venous blood-currents, and then returns to the kneading of the muscles,--and each part is finished by light yet firm upward stroking, the hand returning downward more lightly, yet without breaking its contact with the skin.

Care must be taken as the different groups of muscles are treated that the leg is placed in the position which will most completely relax the ones to be operated upon. Any tension of muscles wholly defeats the effort of the masseur.

After completing the process upon both legs, the arm is next treated in the same manner, the hand receiving somewhat more detailed attention than the foot. Pains must be taken to reach the several groups of the forearm by operating from both sides of the arm. The ordinary manipulation of the shoulder can be accomplished with the patient lying down; but if special conditions, such as articular stiffening, call for unusual care or unusual force, it will be found best to treat the shoulder with the patient seated. The treatment of the arms is concluded with upward stroking (***effleurage***), as with the leg.

In the order usually pursued, the back is the next region treated. The patient lies prone, folding the arms under the head; a firm pillow is put under the epigastric region, so as to the better relax the back muscles, which are too tense when a person lies flat. Beginning from the occiput, both hands stroke firmly and rapidly downward and outward to the spines of the scapulae, at first lightly, then with increasing force. Then the whole back is vigorously rubbed--scrubbed one might call it--with up-and-down strokes, as a preliminary application. The erector spinae masses are treated by careful finger-tip kneading. Working from the spine outward to the axillary line, the muscles of the ribs are acted upon with flat-hand rubbing. The groups of the upper back and shoulder-blades are kneaded and squeezed, the arms being partly abducted so as to separate the shoulder-blades and allow the operator to reach the muscles underlying them. The lumbar regions receive their manipulation last. If it is desirable to give special attention or an extra share of manipulation to any part of the spinal region, this is done as the physician may have ordered, and the whole process is completed by downward friction over the spine, given vigorously and as rapidly as possible.

The chest is the next region to be handled, the patient turning from the prone to the supine position. In women the breasts are usually best left untouched unless special conditions demand their treatment.

The last and perhaps most important part of the process of general massage is the rubbing of the abdomen. Particular care is needed to secure complete relaxation, as nervous patients and, still more, hysterical patients are apt to present extreme rigidity of the abdominal muscles. The head is raised by pillows, the knees are slightly flexed and sometimes supported by a folded pillow also. With this position the rigidity generally yields to gentle persistence, at any rate after a few treatments. If it does not do so, a lateral decubitus may be tried, a position in which the intestinal regions may be very thoroughly treated, and in which, if there be gastric dilatation, the stomach-walls can be best reached. Sweeping circular frictions about the navel as a centre begin the process; the abdominal walls are then kneaded and pinched[16] with one or both hands; deep, firm kneading of the whole belly with the heel of the hand follows, the movements following the course of the colon. Next, the fingers of one hand are all held together in a pyramidal fashion and thrust firmly and slowly into the abdomen, in ordinary cases both hands being used thus alternately, in fat or resisting abdomens one hand pressing upon and aiding the other, and travelling thus over the ascending, transverse, and descending colon. To conclude, the whole belly is shaken by a rapid vibratory motion of the hands (to which is sometimes added succussion by slapping with the flat or cupped hand), and the whole process ends with quick, circular rubbing of the surface.

In cases of troublesome constipation or where other special indications exist, treatment of the abdomen may be much extended beyond the limits here suggested, and indeed it must be remembered that the process of "general massage" as described is capable of a great variety of useful modification to meet individual needs, and is so modified daily by the careful physician and the watchful masseur. It would not be possible or desirable here to describe all the movements which a skilful rubber makes in his treatment, and I have only attempted a skeleton-statement. It will perhaps be noticed by those familiar with the technique of massage that nothing is here said about the use of the movements classed under the general head of "tapotement," the tapping and slapping motions. They have no proper place in the treatment of cases of nervousness, and usually will serve only to irritate and annoy the patient, and often greatly to increase the nervous excitement. Their routine use or over-use constitutes one of the defects of the system of massage as usually practised by the Swedish operators; and when patients tell me, as many do, that "they cannot stand massage," it is often found that the performance of a great deal of this useless and fretting manipulation has constituted a great part of the treatment, and that deep, thorough, quiet kneading can be perfectly borne.

A few precautions are necessary to observe. The grasping hand should carry the skin with it, not slip over the skin, as the drag thus put upon the hairs will, if daily repeated, cause troublesome boils. The use of a lubricant avoids this, and is a favorite device of unskilful manipulators. It also does away with much of the good effected by skin-friction, is uncleanly, very annoying to many patients, promotes an unsightly growth of hair, and should be avoided except where it is desired to rub into the system some oleaginous material. There are exceptional cases where a very dry, harsh skin or a tendency to excessive sweating during massage makes the use of some unguent desirable. Cocoa-oil may be used, or what is perhaps more agreeable, lanolin softened to the consistency of very thick cream by the addition of oil of sweet almonds. As little as possible should be made to serve.

Too much care cannot be used to cover with stockings and warm wraps the parts after in turn they have been subjected to massage. As to time, at first the massage should last half an hour, but should be increased in a week to a full hour. I observe that Dr. Playfair has it used twice a day or more, and I have since had it so employed in some cases, letting the masseuse come before noon, and allowing the nurse to use it at night if it does not interfere with sleep, which is a matter to be tested solely by experiment. Commonly, one hour once daily suffices. I was at one time in the habit of suspending the use of both massage and electricity during menstruation, because I found occasionally that these agents disturbed or checked the normal flow. Of late, however, I continue to employ both agents, but confine them to the limbs. I have met with rare cases in which almost any massage gave rise to a uterine hemorrhage, and in which the utmost caution became necessary.

Women who have a sensitive abdominal surface or ovarian tenderness have of course to be handled with care, but in a few days a practised rubber will by degrees intrude upon the tender regions, and will end by kneading them with all desirable force. The same remarks apply to the spine when it is hurt by a touch; and it is very rare indeed to find persons whose irritable spots cannot at last be rubbed and kneaded to their permanent profit.

Sometimes when the patient is found to be much exhausted by massage, it is well to give some stimulating concentrated food afterwards; occasionally it may be necessary both before and after. In this case it would be well to see that the rubbing was not being made too severe.

Very rarely I find a patient to whom all massage is so disagreeable or produces such annoying nervousness as to make manipulation impossible; sometimes, though very rarely, massage, especially frictional movements, causes sexual excitement when applied in the neighborhood of the genital organs, or even on the buttocks and lower spine, and this may occur in either sane or insane patients: if the rubber observe any signs of this, it will of course be best to avoid handling the areas which are thus sensitive.

Another complaint sometimes made is of chilliness after treatment, and especially of cold feet. If this is not lessened after a few days, the lower extremities may be rubbed last instead of first, or as is now and then useful, the whole order of massage may be changed so as to begin with the abdomen, chest, and upper extremities and conclude with the back and legs.[17]

Beginning with half an hour and gradually increasing to about an hour (a little more for very large or very fat people,--a little less for the small or thin) the daily massage is kept up through at least six weeks, and then if everything seems to be going along well, I direct the rubber or nurse to spend half of the hour in exercising the limbs as a preparation for walking. This is done after the Swedish plan, by making very slowly passive and extreme extensions and flexions of the limbs for a few days, then assisted movements, next active unassisted movements, and last active movements gently resisted by nurse or masseuse. When the patient is able to sit and stand, it is well to keep up and extend the number of these gentle gymnastic acts and to encourage the patient to make them habitual, or at least to keep them up for many months after the conclusion of treatment.[18]

At the seventh week massage is used on alternate days, and is commonly laid aside when the patient gets up and begins to move about.

In 1877, several of the members of the staff of the Infirmary for Nervous Disease, and especially my colleague, Dr. Wharton Sinkler, obliged me by studying with care the influence of massage on temperature, and some very interesting results were obtained. In general, when a highly hysterical person is rubbed, the legs are apt to grow cold under the stimulation, and if this continues to be complained of it is no very good omen of the ultimate success of the treatment. But usually in a few days a change takes place, and the limbs all grow warm when kneaded, as happens in most people from the beginning of the treatment.[19] The extremely low temperature of the limbs of children suffering with so-called essential paralysis is well known. I have frequently seen these strangely cold parts rise, under an hour's massage, six to ten degrees F. In such small limbs, the long contact of a warm hand may account for at least a part of this notable rise in temperature. In adults this can hardly be looked upon as a cause of the rise of temperature produced by massage, first, because the long exposure of large surfaces incident to the process is calculated to lessen whatever increase of heat the contact of the hand may cause, and secondly, because this rise is a very variable quantity, and because occasionally some other and less comprehensible factors actually induce a fall rather than a rise in the thermometer as a result of massage.

In very nervous or hysterical women, ignorant of what the act of kneading may be expected to bring about, and especially in such as are thin and anaemic and have either a somewhat high or an unusually low normal temperature, we may find at first a slight fall of the thermometer, then a fairly constant rise, with some irregularities, and at last, as the health improves, a lessening effect or none at all.

The most notable rise is to be found in persons who, owing to some organic disease, have acquired liability to great changes of temperature.

It is impossible to observe the increase of heat which follows both massage and electricity without inferring that these agents must for a time, like exercise and other tonics, increase the tissue-waste by the stimulus they cause of the general and interstitial circulations, and by the direct influence they seem to have on the tissues themselves. I have sought to study this matter carefully by placing patients on a fixed and competent diet of milk alone, and by estimating the waste of tissues as shown in the secretions before and after the use of massage. This study, although it was never completed in a satisfactory manner, would seem to show that massage does not much alter the total elimination of the entire day, but causes a large and abrupt increase within three hours, followed by a compensatory decline.[20]

I add a number of tables, which very well illustrate the facts above stated as to rise of temperature.

Mrs. J., at rest, on the usual diet. Manipulation at 11, daily:

Before Massage.	After Massage.
100	100
100	100-1/5
99-2/5	99-4/5
99-4/5	100
99-2/5	100
100	100
99-4/5	100
99-4/5	100

Miss P., aet. 24, hysteria:

Before Massage.	After Massage.
99-1/4	99-1/4
98-1/4	99
98-1/2	99
98-1/4	99
98-1/4	98-1/4
99	99-3/4
100-1/5	100-2/5
100-2/5	101-2/5
100-2/5	100-3/5
100-3/5	100

Mrs. L., a very thin, feeble, and bloodless woman, aet. 29 years:

Before Massage.	After Massage.
99	100
98-1/2	99-1/5
98	98-2/5
99	100
98-2/5	98-4/5
99	99-4/5
100	100-1/5
99	99-4/5

Mrs. P., aet. 31, feeble and anaemic, nervous, slight albuminuria and chronic bronchitis. Liable to fever. 3 P.M.:

Before Massage.	After Massage.
101-3/5	102
100	100-4/5
99	99-4/5
100	101
99-2/5	100-1/5
99-4/5	100-3/5
100-3/5	101-3/5
100-2/5	99-4/5
100-3/5	100-2/5
100-3/10	100-9/10
99-1/5	99-4/5

These temperatures were taken always before 4 P.M., and at intervals of three days. Her morning temperature was usually 99 deg. to 99-4/5 deg., and in the evening, 9 to 10 o'clock, it always rose to 100 deg., 101 deg., and at times to 102 deg..

As I have said already, there are persons who, under circumstances seemingly alike, have from massage a large rise of temperature, and others who experience none. I give a single case of what is rare but not exceptional,--an almost constant fall of temperature.

Miss N., aet. 21, hysteria, good condition:

Before Massage.	After Massage.
98	97-3/5
98-1/2	98-1/2
98	98
98-2/5	98
98-4/5	98

These facts are, of course, extremely interesting; but it is well to add that the success of the treatment is not indicated in any constant way by the thermal changes, which are neither so steady nor so remarkable as those caused by electricity.

If now we ask ourselves why massage does good in cases of absolute rest, the answer--at least a partial answer--is not difficult. The secretions of the skin are stimulated by the treatment of that tissue, and it is visibly flushed, as it ought to be, from time to time, by ordinary active exercise. Under massage the flabby muscles acquire a certain firmness, which at first lasts only for a few minutes, but which after a time is more enduring and ends by becoming permanent. The firm grasp of the manipulator's hand stimulates the muscle, and, if sudden, may cause it to contract sensibly, which, however, is not usually desirable or agreeable. The muscles are by these means exercised without the use of volitional exertion or the aid of the nervous centres, and at the same time the alternate grasp and relaxation of the manipulator's hands squeezes out the blood and allows it to flow back anew, thus healthfully exciting the vessels and increasing mechanically the flow of blood to the tissues which they feed. It is possible also that a real increase in the production of red corpuscles is brought about by repeated applications of massage, as will be seen later on.

The visible results as regards the surface-circulation are sufficiently obvious, and most remarkably so in persons who, besides being anaemic and thin, have been long unused to exercise. After a few treatments the nails become pink, the veins show where before none were to be seen, the larger vessels grow fuller, and the whole tint of the body changes for the better.

In like manner the sore places which previously existed, or which were brought into sensitive prominence by the manipulation, by degrees cease to be felt, and a general sensation of comfort and ease follows the later treatments.

Although this plan of acting on the muscles seems to dispense with any demands upon the centres, it is not to be supposed that it is altogether without influence on these parts. In fact, extreme use of massage occasionally flushes the face and causes sense of fulness in the head or ache in the back. The actual large increase in the number of corpuscles in the circulation brought about by massage may be one of the reasons for this. We have added, perhaps, millions of cells to the number in the vessels in a very short time, and need not be astonished if some signs of plethora follow. Moreover, in some spinal maladies it has effects not to be altogether explained by its mechanical stimulation of the muscles, nerves, and skin.

That the deep circulation shares in the changes which are so obvious in the superficial vessels has been shown by various observers of experimental and clinical facts. Firm deep muscle-kneading of the general surface will almost always slow and strengthen the pulse. If the abdomen alone is thoroughly rubbed the same effect appears in the pulse, but less in degree, and massage of the abdomen has also a distinct effect in increasing the flow of urine, a fact worth remembering in cases of heart-disease. In a case of albuminuria from exercise, W.W. Keen has shown that massage did not cause the return of the albumin after rest, though exercise did, a difference due to the opposite effects upon blood-pressure of the two forms of activity. Lauder-Brunton has shown that more blood passes through a masseed part after treatment. Dr. Eccles and Dr. Douglas Graham both found a decided decrease in the circumference of a limb after massage, showing how completely the veins must have been emptied, for the time at least,--an emptying which would surely be followed by an increased flow of arterial blood into the treated region. Dr. J.K. Mitchell, in 1894,[21] made a large number of examinations of the blood before and after massage, some in patients under treatment for a variety of disorders affecting the integrity of the blood, and a few in perfectly healthy men. With scarcely an exception there was a large increase in the number of corpuscles in a cubic millimetre, and an increase, though of less extent, in the haemoglobin-content. Studies made at various intervals after treatment showed that the increase was greatest at the end of about an hour, after which it slowly decreased again; but this decrease was postponed longer and longer when the manipulation was continued regularly as a daily measure.[22] The author's conclusions from these examinations were interesting, and I quote them somewhat fully. The fact that the haemoglobin is less decidedly increased than the corpuscular elements makes it seem at least probable that what happens is, that in all the conditions in which anaemia is a feature there are globules which are not doing their duty, but which are called out by the necessities of increased circulatory activity brought about by massage. If this is the first effect, yet as it is observed that the increase of corpuscles, at first passing, soon becomes permanent, we must conclude that massage has the ultimate effect of stimulating the production of red corpuscles.

One sometimes hears doubts expressed whether a patient with a high-grade anaemia is not "too feeble for such strong treatment" as massage. This study of one of the ways in which massage affects such cases may fairly be taken as proof of the certainty and safety of its effect on them, provided always it be done properly and with intelligence. Some check upon this may be had, as is said elsewhere, by the general effect upon the patient. It may be repeated that the pulse should be slower and stronger after an hour of deep massage, and that this effect will not be produced by superficial rubbing (indeed, with light or too rapid manipulation the pulse may become both less strong and more rapid), and finally the flow of urine should be increased. With these easily observed facts to aid, it may readily be judged whether massage is being rightly applied or not without the need of a visit from the physician during the hour of treatment. A final test might readily be made by examination of the blood and counting the red corpuscles before and after treatment. No doubt in very bad cases a small increase or none would be found at first, but a week of daily manipulation should show a distinct addition to the blood count. A striking instance in which this examination was repeatedly made is related on p. 184.

"It is evident that our present definitions of anaemia are insufficient. An essential part of the description in all of them is that there are defects of number, of color, or of both in the blood. This is not necessarily or always true. The fault may lie in a lack of activity or of availability in the corpuscles. The state of things in the system may be like the want of circulating money during times of panic, when gold is hoarded and not made use of, and interference with commerce and manufactures results.

"Neither an anaemic appearance nor a blood-count is alone enough for a certain diagnosis. Other signs must be used as a check on the blood examination for the establishment of the existence of anaemia. For instance, many cases here recorded had full normal or even supra-normal corpuscle-count, with a good percentage of haemoglobin. Yet they presented every external sign of poverty of blood: pallor of skin and, more important still, of mucous membranes, cold extremities, anorexia, indigestion, dyspnoea on trifling exertion. In such cases we must suppose either that the total volume of the blood is reduced, or that the usefulness of the corpuscles is in some way impaired, or that both these troubles exist together."[23]

I have said above that the face was not touched in the course of the rubbing. There are cases, however, in which massage of the head and face may be usefully practised. Some obstinate neuralgias are helped by it temporarily, and very often it is of use with other means to aid in a permanent cure. Many headaches of a passing character may be dissipated promptly by careful massage of the head or by downward stroking over the jugular veins at the sides of the neck to lessen the flow of blood into the cerebral vessels, where the pain is due to congestion or distention, and careful manipulation of the facial muscles in paralysis is of service in restoring loss of tone and improving their nutrition. It is worth adding here, as women patients frequently say that during their illness the hair has become thin or shown a great tendency to fall, that daily firm finger-tip massage of the head for ten or twelve minutes, followed by rubbing into the scalp of a small amount of a tonic, either a bland oil or if need be of some more stimulating material, will in a great majority of the instances where loss of hair is due to general ill-health perfectly restore its vigor and even its color.

I am accustomed to pay a good deal of attention to the observations made on these and other points by practised manipulators, and I find that their daily familiarity with every detail of the color, warmth, and firmness of the tissues is of great use to me.

A great deal of nonsense is talked and written as to the use and the usefulness of massage. The "professional rubber" not unnaturally makes a mystery of it, and patients talk foolishly about "magnetism" and "electricity;" but what is needed is a strong, warm, soft hand, directed by ordinary intelligence and instructed by practice; and this is the whole of the matter, except in the massage of such obscure conditions as need full knowledge of the anatomical relations and physiological functions of the parts to be rubbed. It is a fact that I have known country physicians who, desiring to use massage and not having a practitioner of it within reach, have themselves trained persons to do it, with considerable resultant success.

It is not, perhaps, putting it too strongly to say that bad massage is better than none in those cases in which manipulation is needed. Very little harm can result from its use even by unskilled hands, provided that reasonable intelligence direct them.

CHAPTER VII.
ELECTRICITY.

Electricity is the second means which I have made use of for the purpose of exercising muscles in persons at rest. It has also an additional value, of which I shall presently speak.

In order to exercise the muscles best and with the least amount of pain and annoyance, we make use of an induction current, with interruptions as slow as one in every two to five seconds, a rate readily obtained in properly-constructed batteries.[24] This plan is sure to give painless exercise, but it is less rapid and less complete as to the quality of the exercise caused than the movements evolved by very rapid interruptions. These, in the hands of a clever operator who knows his anatomy well, are therefore, on the whole, more satisfactory, but they require some experience to manage them so as not to shock and disgust the patient by inflicting needless pain. The poles, covered with absorbent cotton well wetted with salt water, which may be readily changed, so as not to use the same material more than once, are placed on each muscle in turn, and kept about four inches apart. They are moved fast enough to allow of the muscles being well contracted, which is easily managed, and with sufficient speed, if the assistant be thoroughly acquainted with the points of Ziemssen. The smaller electrode should cover the motor-point and the larger be used upon an indifferent area. After the legs are treated, the muscles of the belly and back and loins are gone over systematically, and finally those of the chest and arms. The face and neck are neglected. About forty minutes to an hour are needed; but at first a less time is employed. The general result is to exercise in turn all the external muscles.[25]

No such obvious and visible results are seen as we observe after massage, but the thermal changes are much more constant and remarkable, and show at least that we are not dealing with an agent which merely amuses the patient or acts alone through some mysterious influence on the mental status.

A half-hour's treatment of the muscles commonly gives rise to a marked elevation of temperature, which fades away within an hour or two. This effect is, like that from massage, most notable in persons liable to fever from some organic trouble, and it varies as to its degree in individuals who have no such disease.

The first case, Miss B., aet. 20, is an example of tubercular disease of the apex of the right lung. She had a morning temperature of 98-1/2 deg. to 99-1/2 deg., and an evening temperature of 100 deg. to 102 deg.

Electricity was used about 11 o'clock daily, with these results:

	Before Electricity.	After Electricity.
November 25	99	99-3/5
" 27	97-3/5	100
" 28	98	99
" 29	98-4/5	99-4/5
December 2	100-1/5	101-3/5
" 4	99-1/5	100-1/5
" 5	99-2/5	99-1/5

Mrs. R., aet. 40, the next case, was merely a rather anaemic, feeble, and thin woman, who for years had not been able to endure any prolonged effort. She got well under the general treatment, gaining thirteen pounds on a weight of ninety-eight pounds, her height being five feet and one inch. The facts as to rise of temperature are most remarkable, and, I need not say, were carefully observed.

Temperature taken in the mouth while at rest in bed.

	Before Electricity.	After Electricity.
April 2	98-2/5	98-4/5
" 3	98-1/5	98-2/5
" 4	98-1/5	98-2/5
" 5	98	98-3/5
" 6	97-9/10	98-7/10
" 7	98	98-5/10
" 8	98	98-3/5
" 9	98	98-1/10
" 10	98-2/5	98-3/5
" 11	98-5/10	98-7/10
" 12	98-3/5	99-1/10
" 13	98-1/5	99-5/10
" 14	98-2/5	99-1/5
" 16	98-4/10	99-1/10
" 17	98-5/10	99-2/10
" 18	98-7/10	99-1/10 One hour later, 99-1/10
" 19	98-9/10	99-3/10 " " " , 98-4/5

	Before Electricity.	After Electricity.
April 20	99	99-1/10
" 21	98-9/10	99-2/10
	Menstrual period.	
" 30	98-3/5	98-3/5
May 1	98	98-5/10
" 2	98	98-3/10

The third case, Miss M., aet. 33, was that of a pallid woman, the daughter of a well-known physician in the South. She suffered for six years with "nervous exhaustion," headaches, pain in the back, intense depression of spirits, nausea, and repeated attacks of hysteria. She slept only under anodynes, and used stimulants freely. Under the use of rest and the adjuvant treatment described, Miss M. made a thorough recovery, and was restored to useful active life.

Miss M. Thermometer held in mouth.

	Before Electricity.	After Electricity.
May 14	99-1/10	99-1/10 } Menstruating; general } faradization only.
" 15	99	99-1/5 }
" 16	99-1/5	99-1/5 Gen'l faradization and limbs.
" 17	98-4/5	99-1/5
" 18	98-4/5	99-1/5
" 19	98-1/5	98-4/5
" 21	98-3/5	99
" 22	98-4/5	99-1/10

	Before Electricity.	After Electricity.
May 25	98-1/10	98-4/10
" 26	98-1/10	99-1/10
" 29	98-3/5	99
" 30	98-5/10	99-1/10
" 31	98-9/10	99-1/10

Mrs. P., aet. 38, was a rather nervous woman, easily tired, but not anaemic and not very thin. She improved greatly under the treatment.

	Before Electricity.	After Electricity.	
January 27	98-3/5	99-1/5	Thermometer in axilla ten
" 29	98-2/5	99-1/5	minutes before and after.
" 30	99-1/5	99-3/5	
" 31	98-4/5	99-2/5	
February 1	99	99-2/5	
	Menstrual period.		
February 8	98-2/5	99-1/5	
" 9	98-3/5	99	
" 10	98-2/5	99	

		Before Electricity.	After Electricity.
"	12	98-1/5	99-3/5
"	13	98-2/5	99
"	14	98-2/5	98-3/5
"	15	98-2/5	98-4/5
"	19	99	98-2/5
"	20	98	99
"	23	98-3/5	99-4/5 Thermometer in mouth five
"	24	99	99-2/5 minutes before and after.
"	27	99-1/5	99-3/5
"	28	98-4/5	99-4/5

Menstrual period.

Menstrual period.

		Before Electricity.	After Electricity.
March 13		99	99-2/5
"	14	98-4/5	98-4/5
"	15	99	99-1/5

Miss R., aet. 27, was a fair case of hysterical conditions; over-use of chloral and bromides; anorexia and loss of flesh and color.

Thermometer in mouth.

	Before Electricity.	After Electricity.	
May 15	100	100	}
			} General faradization
" 16	100	100	} for fifteen minutes.
			}
" 17	100-1/5	100-2/5 }	
" 18	98-2/5	98-3/5 } General faradization,	
		} fifteen minutes, also of	
" 19	99-4/5	100-1/10 } arm muscles,	
		twenty minutes.	
May 20	100-1/10	100	
			General faradization, ten
" 22	99-2/5	99-3/5	minutes; arms and legs
			twenty minutes.
" 26	99-1/10	99-2/10	
" 27	99-3/10	99-4/10	
" 28	99-2/5	99-2/5	
" 29	99-3/10	99-3/10	
" 30	99-1/10	99-4/10	
" 31	99-1/10	99-2/10	

June	2	99-3/5	99-4/5
"	4	99-5/10	99-6/10
"	6	99-3/10	99-5/10
"	7	99-3/10	99-5/10

I have given these full details because I have not seen elsewhere any statement of the rather remarkable phenomena which they exemplify. It may be that a part at least of the thermal change is due to the muscular action, although this seems hardly competent to account for any large share in the alteration of temperature, and we must look further to explain it fully. No mental excitement can be called upon as a cause, since it continues after the patient is perfectly accustomed to the process. I should add, also, that in most cases the subject of the experiment was kept in ignorance of the fact that a rise of the thermometer was to be expected. Is it not possible that the current even of an induction battery has the power so to stimulate the tissues as to cause an increase in the ordinary rate of disintegrative change? Perhaps a careful study of the secretions might lend force to this suggestion. That the muscular action produced by the battery is not essential to the increase of bodily heat is shown by the next set of facts to which I desire to call attention.

Some years ago, Messrs. Beard and Rockwell stated that when an induced current is used for fifteen to thirty minutes daily, one pole on the neck and one on either foot, or alternately on both, the persistent use of this form of treatment is decidedly tonic in its influence. I believe that in this opinion they were perfectly correct, and I am now able to show that, when thus employed, the induced current causes also a decided rise of temperature in many people, which proves at least that it is in some way an active agent, capable of positively influencing the nutritive changes of the body.

The rise of temperature thus caused is less constant, as well as less marked, than that occasioned by the muscle treatment. I do not think it necessary to give the tables in full. They show in the best cases, rises of one-fifth to four-fifths of a degree

F., and were taken with the utmost care to exclude all possible causes of error.

The mode of treatment is as follows: At the close of the muscle-electrization one pole is placed on the nape of the neck and one on a foot for fifteen minutes. Then the foot pole is shifted to the other foot and left for the same length of time.

The primary current is used, as being less painful, and the interruptions are made as rapid as possible, while the cylinder or control wires are adjusted so as to give a current which is not uncomfortable.

It is desirable to have electricity used by a practised hand, but of late I have found that intelligent nurses may suffice, and this, of course, materially lessens the cost. In very timid or nervous people, or those who at some time have been severely "shocked" by the application of electricity in the hands of charlatans, it is common to find the patient greatly dreading a return to its use. In this case, if the battery be started and the poles moved about on the surface as usual, but without any connection being made, one of two things will happen,--either the patient will naturally find it very mild, and will submit fearlessly to a gentle and increasing treatment, or else her apprehensions will so dominate her as to cause her to complain of the effects as exciting or tiring her, or as spoiling her sleep. A few words of kindly explanation will suffice to show her how much expectation has to do with the apparent results, and she will be found, if the matter be managed with tact, to have learned a lesson of wide usefulness throughout her treatment.

However, there are occasional, though very rare, cases in which it is impossible to use faradism at all by reason of the insomnia and nervousness which result even after very careful and gentle application of the current. On the other hand, some patients find the effect of the electric application so soothing as to promote sleep, and will ask to have it repeated or regularly given in the evening.

I have been asked very often if all the means here described be necessary, and I have been criticised by some of the reviewers of my first edition because I had not pointed out the relative needfulness of the various agencies employed. In fact, I have made very numerous clinical studies of cases, in some of which I used rest, seclusion, and massage, and in others rest, seclusion, and electricity. It is, of course, difficult, I may say impossible, to state in any numerical manner the reason for my conclusion in favor of the conjoined use of all these means. If one is to be left out, I have no hesitation in saying that it should be electricity.

CHAPTER VIII.
DIETETICS AND THERAPEUTICS.

The somewhat wearisome and minute details I have given as to seclusion, rest, massage, and electricity have prepared the way for a discussion of the dietetic and medicinal treatment which without them would be neither possible nor useful.

As to diet, we have to be guided somewhat by the previous condition and history of the patient.

It is difficult to treat any of these cases without a resort at some time more or less to the use of milk. In most dyspeptic cases--and few neurasthenic women fail to be obstinately dyspeptic--milk given at the outset, and given alone by Karell's method for a fortnight or less, enormously simplifies our treatment. Even after that, milk is the best and most easily managed addition to a general diet. As to its use with rest and massage as an exclusive diet in obesity alone or in extreme fatness with anaemia, I spoke in a former edition with a confidence which has been increased by the added experience of physicians on both sides of the Atlantic. Finally, there are exceptional cases of intestinal pain of obscure parentage or seemingly neuralgic, of dyspepsia incorrigible by other treatments, which, having resulted in grave general defects of nutrition, are best treated by several weeks of milk diet, combined with rest, massage, and electricity. Milk, therefore, must be so much used in these cases in connection with the general treatment I am describing that it is perhaps as well to say more clearly how it is to be employed when given alone or with other food. I am the more willing to do this because I have learned certain facts as to the effects of milk diet which have, I believe, hitherto escaped observation. In fact, the study of the therapeutic influence and full results of exclusive diets is yet to be made; nor can I but believe that accurate dietetics will come to be a far more useful part of our means of managing certain cases than as yet seems possible.

We are indebted chiefly to Dr. Karell, of St. Petersburg, for our knowledge of the value of milk as an exclusive diet, and to Dr. Donkin for the extension of Karell's treatment to diabetes. I shall formulate as curtly as possible the rules to be followed in using milk as an exclusive diet in dyspeptic states, and in anaemia with obesity, and in the latter state uncomplicated by defective haemic conditions.

For fuller statements as to the reasons for the various rules to be observed in using milk, I must refer the reader to Karell's paper and to Donkin's book.

Have the utmost care used as to preservation of the milk employed, and as to the perfect cleansing of all vessels in which it is kept. Use well-skimmed milk, as fresh as can be had, and, if possible, let it be obtained from the cow twice a day. Or if this is not possible, or where any doubt exists as to the condition of the milk, or any difficulty is experienced in keeping it fresh, it may be pasteurized as soon as received by heating it to 160 deg., keeping it some minutes at this point, and at once chilling on ice. For this purpose it is best to have the milk in bottles, and to heat by immersing the bottles in a water-bath. For longer preservation, as, for example, when travelling, sterilizing may be more thoroughly done by greater heat and lengthened immersion. Still, these should be expedients for use only when milk cannot be secured fresh and in good order, as it is more than doubtful if the milk is so well borne when it has been altered by these processes.

For ordinary daily use it might be better to let all the milk for the day be peptonized in the morning with pancreatic extract, to the extent which is found to be agreeable to the patient's taste, and then preserve it by placing it upon ice. In this way milk may be kept for several days. Then, too, it has been found that where even skimmed milk upsets the stomach of patients, milk prepared in this manner can be taken without trouble. In peptonizing, the directions which accompany the powders to be used for that purpose should be followed carefully. It is to be remembered that if the patient desires to take the milk warm, the process of conversion into peptones, which has been stopped by the cold, will be promptly started again when the fluid is warmed, and then a very few minutes will suffice to make it disagreeably bitter. At first the skimming should be thorough, and for the treatment of dyspepsia or albuminuria the milk must be as creamless as possible. The milk of the common cow is, for our purposes, preferable to that of the Alderney. It may be used warm or cold, but, except in rare cases of diarrhoea, should not be boiled.

It ought to be given at least every two hours at first, in quantities not to exceed four ounces, and as the amount taken is enlarged, the periods between may be lengthened, but not beyond three hours during the waking day, the last dose to be used at bedtime or near it. If the patient be wakeful, a glass should be left within reach at night, and always its use should be resumed as early as possible in the morning. A little lime-water may be added to the night milk, to preserve it sweet, and it should be kept covered.

The milk given during the day should be taken at set times, and very slowly sipped in mouthfuls; and this is an important rule in many cases. Where it is so disagreeable as to cause great disgust or nausea, the addition of enough of tea or coffee or caramel or salt to merely flavor it may enable us to make its use bearable, and we may by degrees abandon these aids. Another plan, rarely needed, is to use milk with the general diet and lessen the latter until only milk is employed. If these rules be followed, it is rare to find milk causing trouble; but if its use give rise to acidity, the addition of alkalies or lime-water may help us, or these may be used and the milk scalded by adding a fourth of boiling water to the milk, which has been previously put in a warm glass. Some patients digest it best when it has the addition of a teaspoonful of barley-or rice-water to each ounce, the main object being to prevent the formation of large, firm clots in the stomach,--an end which may also be attained by the addition at the moment of drinking of a little carbonated water from a siphon. For the sake of variety, buttermilk may be substituted for a portion of the fresh milk, and though less nourishing it has the advantage of being mildly laxative.

When used as an exclusive diet, skimmed milk gives rise to certain very interesting and what I might call normal symptoms. Since at first we can rarely give enough to sustain the functions, for several days the patient is apt to lose weight, which is another reason why exercise is in such cases undesirable. This loss soon ceases, and in the end there is usually a gain, while in most rest cases an exclusive milk diet may be dispensed with after a week. Where milk is taken alone for weeks or months, it is common enough to observe a large increase in bodily weight. I have seen several times active men, even laboring men, live for long periods on milk, with no loss of weight; but large quantities have to be used,--two and a half to three gallons daily. A gentleman, a diabetic, was under my observation for fifteen years, during the whole of which time he took no other food but milk and carried on a large and prosperous business. Milk may, therefore, be safely asserted to be a sufficient food in itself, even for an adult, if only enough of it be taken.

During the first week or two, exclusive milk diet gives rise to a marked sense of sleepiness. It causes nearly always, and even for weeks of its use, a white and thick fur on the tongue, and often for a time an unpleasant sweetish taste in the early morning, neither of which need be regarded. Intense constipation and yellowish stools of a peculiar odor are usual. Of the former I shall speak in connection with the use of milk in special cases. The influence of milk on the urinary secretion is more remarkable, and has not been as yet fully studied.

There is, of course, a large flow of urine; and in dropsical cases due to renal maladies this may exceed the ingested fluid and carry away very rapidly the dropsical accumulations. It is sometimes annoying to nervous persons because of the frequent micturition it makes necessary. I have discovered that while skimmed milk alone is being taken, uric acid usually disappears almost entirely from the urine, so that it is difficult to discover even a trace of this substance; nor does it seem to return so long as nothing but creamless milk is used. Almost any large addition of other food, but especially of meat, enables us to find it again. Creatine and creatinine also seem to lessen in amount, but of the extent of this change I am not as yet fully informed.

A yet more singular alteration occurs as to the pigments. If after a fortnight or less of exclusive milk diet we fill with the urine a long test-tube, and, placing it beside a similar tube of the ordinary urine of an adult, look down into the two tubes, we shall observe that the milk urine has a singular greenish tint, which once seen cannot again be mistaken. If we put some of this urine in a test-tube carefully upon hot nitric acid, there is noticed none of the usual brown hue of oxidized pigment at the plane of contact. In fact, it is often difficult to see where the two fluids meet.

The precise nature of this greenish-yellow pigment has not, I believe, been made out; but it seems clear that during a diet of milk the ordinary pigments of the urine disappear or are singularly modified. A single meal of meat will at once cause their return for a time.

These results have been carefully re-examined at my request by Dr. Marshall in the Laboratory of the University of Pennsylvania, and his results and my own have been found to accord; while he has also discovered that during the use of milk the substances which give rise to the ordinary faecal odors disappear, and are replaced by others the nature of which is not as yet fully comprehended. The changes I have here pointed out are remarkable indications of the vast alterations in assimilation and in the destruction of tissues which seem to take place under the influence of this peculiar diet. Some of them may account for its undoubted value in lithaemic or gouty states; but, at all events, they point to the need for a more exhaustive study both of this and of other methods of exclusive diet.

As regards milk, enough has here been said to act as a guide in its practical use in the class of cases with which we are now concerned; but I may add that it is sometimes useful, as the case progresses, to employ in place of milk, or with it, some one of the various "children's foods," such as Nestle's food, or malted milk.

Before dealing with the treatment of the anaemic and feeble and more or less wasted invalids who require treatment by rest and its concomitant aids, I desire to say a few words as to the use of rest, milk dietetics, and massage in people who are merely cumbrously loaded with adipose tissues, and also in the very small class of anaemic women who are excessively fat and may or may not be hysterical, but are apt to be feeble and otherwise wretched.

Karell has pointed out that on creamless milk diet fat people lose flesh; and this is true; so that sometimes this mode of lessening weight succeeds very well. But it does not always answer, because, as in Banting, loss of weight is apt to be accompanied with loss of strength, so that in some cases the results are disastrous, or at least alarming. I do not know that this is ever the case if the directions of Mr. Harvey[26] are followed with care and the weight very deliberately lessened. But for this few people have the patience; and, even if they can be induced to follow out a strict diet, it is often useful to be able to cut off very rapidly a large amount of weight, and so shorten the period of strict regimen, or at least put over-fat persons in a condition to exercise with a freedom which had become difficult, and thus to provide them with a healthful means of preventing an accumulation of adipose matter. This can be done rapidly and with safety by the following means. The person whose weight we decide to lessen is placed on skimmed milk alone, with the usual precautions; or at once we give skimmed milk with the usual food, and in a week put aside all other diet save milk and all other fluids. When we find what quantity of milk will sustain the weight, we diminish the amount by degrees until the patient is losing a half-pound of weight each day, or less or more, as seems to be well borne. Meanwhile, during the first week or two rest in bed is enjoined, and later for a varying period rest in bed or on a lounge is insisted upon, while at the same time massage is used once or twice a day, and later in the case Swedish movements. At the same time, the pulse and weight are observed with care, so that if there be too rapid loss, or any sign of feebleness, the diet may be increased. In many such cases I allow daily a moderate amount of beef- or chicken- or oyster-soup,--more as a relief to the unpleasantness of a milk diet than for any other reason.

When the weight has been sufficiently lowered, we add to the diet beef, mutton, oysters, etc., and finally arrange a full diet list to include but a moderate amount of hydro-carbons. Meanwhile, the milk remains as a large part of the food, and the active Swedish movements are still kept up as a habit, the patient being directed by degrees to add the usual forms of exercise.

If we attempt to make so speedy a change in weight while the patient is afoot, the loss is apt to be gravely felt; but with the precautions here advised it is interesting and pleasant to see how great a reduction may be made in a reasonable time without annoyance and with no obvious result except a gain in health and comfort.

Cases of anaemia in women with excess of flesh have to be managed in a somewhat similar fashion, but with the utmost care. In such persons we have a loss of red blood-globules, perhaps lessened haemoglobin, weak heart, rapid pulse, and general feebleness, with too much fat, but not, or at least rarely, extreme obesity. The milder cases may profit by iron, with rest and very vigorous massage, but in old cases of this kind--they are, happily, rare--the best plan is to put the patient at rest, to use massage, restrict the diet to skimmed milk, or to milk and broths free from fat, and with them, when the weight has been sufficiently lowered, to give iron freely, and by degrees a good general diet, under which the globules rise in number, so that even with a new gain in flesh there comes an equal gain in strength and comfort. The massage must be very thoroughly done to be of service, and it is often difficult to get operators to perform it properly, as the manipulation of very fat people is excessively hard work. As to other details, the management should be much the same as that which I shall presently describe in connection with cases of another kind.

I add two cases in illustration of the use of rest, milk, and massage in the treatment of persons who are both anaemic and overloaded with fat.

Mrs. P., aet. 45, weight one hundred and ninety pounds, height five feet four and a half inches, had for some years been feeble, unable to walk without panting, or to move rapidly even a few steps. Although always stout, her great increase of flesh had followed an attack of typhoid fever four years before. Her appearance was strikingly suggestive of anaemia.

She was subject to constant attacks of acid dyspepsia, was said to be unable to bear iron in any form, and had not menstruated for seven months. She had no uterine disease, and was not pregnant. Two years before I saw her she had been made very ill owing to an attempt to reduce her flesh by too rapid Banting, and since then, although not a gross or large eater, she had steadily gained in weight, and as steadily in discomfort.

She was kept in bed for five weeks. Massage was used at first once daily, and after a fortnight twice a day, while milk was given, and in a week made the exclusive diet. Her average of loss for thirty days was a pound a day, and the diet was varied by the addition of broths after the third week, so as to keep the reduction within safe limits. Her pulse at first was 90 to 100 in the morning, and at night 80 to 95, her temperature being always a half degree to a degree below the normal. At the third week the latter was as is usual in health, and the pulse had fallen to 80 in the morning, and 80 to 90 at night.

After two weeks I gave her the lactate of iron every three hours in full doses. In the fourth week additions were made to her diet-list, and Swedish movements were added to the massage, which was applied but once a day; and during the fifth week she began to sit up and move about. At the seventh week her pulse was 70 to 80, her temperature natural, and her blood-globules much increased in number. Her weight had now fallen to one hundred and forty-five pounds, and her appearance had decidedly improved. She left me after three and a half months, able to walk with comfort three miles. She has lived, of course, with care ever since, but writes me now, after two years, that she is a well and vigorous woman. Her periodical flow came back five months after her treatment began, and she has since had a child.

Early in the spring of 1876, Mrs. C., aet. 40, came under my care with partial hysterical paralysis of the right and hemi-anaesthesia of the left side. She had no power to feel pain or to distinguish heat from cold in the left leg and arm, though the sense of touch was perfect. The long strain of great mental suffering had left her in this state and rendered her somewhat emotional. Her appetite was fair, but she was strangely white, and weighed one hundred and sixty-three pounds, with a height of five feet five inches. As she had had endless treatment by iron, change of air, and the like, I did not care to repeat what had already failed. She was therefore put at rest, and treated with milk, slowly lessened in amount. Her stomach-troubles, which had been very annoying, disappeared, and when the milk fell to three pints she began to lose flesh. With a quart of milk a day she lost half a pound daily, and in two weeks her weight fell to one hundred and forty pounds. She was then placed on the full treatment which I shall hereafter describe. The weight returned slowly, and with it she became quite ruddy, while her flesh lost altogether its flabby character. I never saw a more striking result.

I have been careful to speak at length of these fat anaemic cases, because, while rare, they have been, to me at least, among the most difficult to manage of all the curable anaemias, and because with the plan described I have been almost as successful as I could desire.

Let us now suppose that we have to deal with a person of another and different type,--one of the larger class of feeble, thin-blooded, neurasthenic or hysterical women. Let us presume that every ordinary and easily attainable means of relief has been utterly exhausted, for not otherwise do I consider it reasonable to use so extreme a treatment as the one we are now to consider. Inevitably, if it be a woman long ill and long treated, we shall have to settle the question of uterine therapeutics. A careful examination is made, and we learn that there is decided displacement. In this case it is well to correct it at once and to let the uterine treatment go on with the general treatment. If there be bad lacerations of the womb or perineum, their surgical relief may await a change in the general status of health,--say at the fourth or fifth week. If there be only congestive or other morbid states of the womb or ovaries, they are best left to be aided by the general gain in health; but in this as in every other stage of this treatment it is unwise, and undesirable therefore, to lay down too absolute laws. Having satisfied ourselves as to these points, and that rest, etc., is needful, we begin treatment, if possible, at the close of a menstrual period, because usually the monthly flow is a time at which there is little or no gain, and by starting our treatment when it is just over we save a week of time in bed.

The next step is, usually, to get her by degrees on a milk diet, which has two advantages. It enables us to know precisely the amount of food taken, and to regulate it easily; and it nearly always dismisses, as by magic, all the dyspeptic conditions. If the case be an old one, I rarely omit the milk; but, although I begin with three or four ounces every two hours, I increase it in a few days up to two quarts, given in divided doses every three hours. If a cup of coffee given without sugar on awaking does not regulate the bowels, I add a small amount of watery extract of aloes at bedtime; or if the constipation be obstinate, I give thrice a day one-quarter of a grain of watery extract of aloes with two grains of dried ox-gall. I find the simple milk diet a great aid towards getting rid of chloral, bromides, and morphia, all of which I usually am able to lay aside during the first week of treatment.[27] Nor is it less easy with the same means to enable the patient to give up stimulus; and I may add that in the treatment of the congested stomach of the habitual hard drinker the milk treatment is of admirable efficacy. As I have spoken over and over of the use of stimulus by nervous women, I should be careful to explain that anything like great excess on the part of women of the upper classes, in this country at least, is, in my opinion, extremely rare, and that when I speak of the habit of stimulation I mean only that nervous women are apt to be taught to take wine or whiskey daily, to an extent that does not affect visibly their appearance or demeanor.

Meanwhile, the mechanical treatment is steadily pursued, and within four days to a week, when the stomach has become comfortable, I order the patient to take also a light breakfast. A day or two later she is given a mutton-chop as a mid-day dinner, and again in a day or two she has added bread-and-butter thrice a day; within ten days I am commonly able to allow three full meals daily, as well as three or four pints of milk, which are given at or after meals, in place of water.

After ten days I order also two to four ounces of fluid malt extract before each meal. The fluid malt extracts which now reach us from Germany have become less trustworthy than they formerly were. Some of them keep badly, and are uncertain in composition, one bottle being good, another bad. The more constant, and at the same time most agreeable, extracts are those now made in this country. Although their diastasic powers are usually less than is claimed for them, and vary greatly even in the best makes, they so far have seemed to me on the whole more satisfactory than the imported malts. It is very desirable that a thorough chemical study should be made of the various malt extracts, solid and liquid. I am sure that some of them are defective in composition, or vary notably as to the amount of alcohol they contain.

No troublesome symptoms usually result from this full feeding, and the patient may be made to eat more largely by being fed by her attendant. People who will eat very little if they feed themselves, often take a large amount when fed by another; and, as I have said before, nothing is more tiresome than for a patient flat on her back to cut up her food and to use the fork or spoon. By the plan of feeding we thus gain doubly.

As to the meals, I leave them to the patient's caprice, unless this is too unreasonable; but I like to give butter largely, and have little trouble in getting this most wholesome of fats taken in large amounts. A cup of cocoa or of coffee with milk on waking in the morning is a good preparation for the fatigue of the toilet.

At the close of the first week I like to add one pound of beef, in the form of raw soup. This is made by chopping up one pound of raw beef and placing it in a bottle with one pint of water and five drops of strong hydrochloric acid. This mixture stands on ice all night, and in the morning the bottle is set in a pan of water at 110 deg. F. and kept two hours at about this temperature. It is then thrown on to a stout cloth and strained until the mass which remains is nearly dry. The filtrate is given in three portions daily. If the raw taste prove very objectionable, the beef to be used is quickly roasted on one side, and then the process is completed in the manner above described. The soup thus made is for the most part raw, but has also the flavor of cooked meat.[28]

In difficult cases, especially those treated in cool weather, I sometimes add, at the third week, one half-ounce of cod-liver oil, given half an hour after each meal. If it lessen the appetite, or cause nausea, I employ it thrice a day as a rectal injection; and in cases where the large doses of iron used cause intense constipation, I find the use of cod-oil enemata doubly valuable, by acting as a nutriment and by disposing the bowels to act daily. This may be given as an emulsion with pancreatic extract. This will suit some people well, and result in a single passage daily, but in others may be annoying, and be either badly retained or not retained at all, and may give rise to tenesmus.

The question of stimulus is a grave one. In too many cases which come to me, I have to give so much care to break off the use of all forms of alcoholic drinks that I am loath to resort to them in any case, although I am satisfied that a small amount is a help towards speedy increase of fat. Its use is, therefore, a matter for careful judgment, and in persons who have never taken it in excess, or as a habit, I prefer to give, with the other treatment, a small daily ration of stimulus: an ounce a day of whiskey in milk, or a glass of dry champagne or red wine, seems to me useful as an adjuvant, and as increasing the capacity to take food at meals. Nevertheless, alcohol is not essential, and for the most part I give none, except the small amount--some four per cent.--present in fluid malt extracts. Even this is found to excite certain persons, and it is in such cases easy to substitute the thicker extracts of malt, or the Japanese extract, made from barley and rice.

So soon as my patient begins to take other food than milk, and sometimes even before this, I like to give iron in large doses. In hospital practice the old subcarbonate answers very well, being cheap, and not unpalatable when shaken up in water or given in an effervescent draught of carbonated waters. In private practice large doses of salts of iron, as four to six grains of lactate at meal-time, are satisfactory; but the form of iron is of less moment than the amount.

Very often I meet with women who cannot take iron, either because it disturbs the stomach, causes headache, or constipates, or else because they have been told never to take iron. In the latter case I simply add five grains of the pyrophosphate to each ounce of malt, and give it thus for a month unknown to the patients. It is then easy to make clear to them that iron is not so difficult to take as they had been led to believe, and when it has ceased to disagree mentally I find that I am able to fall back on the coarser method. If iron constipate, as it may and does often do when used in these large doses, the trouble is to be corrected by fruit, and especially pears, by the pill of the watery extract of aloes and ox-gall already mentioned, by extracts of cascara or of juglans cinerea, which may be added to the malt extract ordered with the meals, or by enemata of oil, or oil and glycerin, or a glycerin suppository. The instances in which iron gives headache and sense of fulness are very rare when the patient is undergoing the full treatment described, and, as a rule, I disregard all such complaints, and find that after a time I cease to hear anything more of these symptoms.

Unless some especial need arises, iron, in some form, is the only drug I care to use until the patient begins to sit up, when I order nearly always sulphate of strychnia, in rather full doses, thrice a day, with iron and arsenic.

Probably no physician will read the account I have here detailed of the vast amount of food which I am enabled to give, not only with impunity from dyspepsia, but with lasting advantage, without some sense of wonder; and, for my own part, I can only say that I have watched again and again with growing surprise some listless, feeble, white-blooded creature learning by degrees to consume these large rations, and gathering under their use flesh, color, and wholesomeness of mind and body. It is needless to say that it is not in all cases easy to carry out this treatment.

When the full treatment has been reached, and kept up for a few days, I begin to watch the urine with care, because if the patient be overfed the renal secretion speedily betrays this result in the precipitation of urates. When this occurs at all steadily, I usually give directions to lessen the amount of food until the urine is again free from sediment.

Nearly always at some time in the progress of the case there are attacks of dyspepsia, when it suffices to cut down the diet one-half, or to give milk alone for a day or two. Diarrhoea is more rare, and has to be met in like manner; or, if obstinate, it may be requisite to give the milk boiled. Occasionally the rapid increase of blood is shown by nasal hemorrhage, which needs no especial treatment.

Perhaps I shall make myself more clear if I now relate in full the diet-list of some of my cases, and the mode of arranging it.

I take the following case as an illustration from my -book:

Mrs. C., a New England woman, aet. 33, undertook, at the age of sixteen, a severe course of mental labor, and within two years completed the whole range of studies which, at the school she went to, were usually spread over four years. An early marriage, three pregnancies, the last two of which broke in upon the years of nursing, began at last to show in loss of flesh and color. Meanwhile, she met with energy the multiplied claims of a life full of sympathy for every form of trouble, and, neglecting none of the duties of society or kinship, yet found time for study and accomplishments. By and by she began to feel tired, and at last gave way quite abruptly, ceased to menstruate five years before I saw her, grew pale and feeble, and dropped in weight in six months from one hundred and twenty-five pounds to ninety-five. Nature had at last its revenge. Everything wearied her,--to eat, to drive, to read, to sew. Walking became impossible, and, tied to her couch, she grew dyspeptic and constipated. The asthenopia which is almost constantly seen in such cases added to her trials, because reading had to be abandoned, and so at last, despite unusual vigor of character, she gave way to utter despair, and became at times emotional and morbid in her views of life. After numberless forms of treatment had been used in vain, she came to this city and passed into my care.

At this time she could not walk more than a few steps without flushing and without a sense of painful tire. Her morning temperature was 97.5 deg. F., and her white corpuscles were perhaps a third too numerous. After most careful examination, I could find no disease of any one organ, and I therefore advised a resort to the treatment by rest, with full confidence in the result.

In this single case I give the schedule of diet in full as a fair example:

Mrs. C. remained in bed in entire repose. She was fed, and rose only for the purpose of relieving the bladder or the rectum.

October 10.--Took one quart of milk in divided doses every two hours.

11th.--A cup of coffee on rising, and two quarts of milk given in divided portions every two hours. A pill of aloes every night, which answered for a few days.

12th to 15th.--Same diet. The dyspepsia by this time was relieved, and she slept without her habitual dose of chloral. The pint of raw soup was added in three portions on the 16th.

17th and 18th.--Same diet.

19th.--She took, on awaking at 7, coffee; at 7.30, a half-pint of milk; and the same at 10 A.M., 12 M., 2, 4, 6, 8, and 10 P.M. The soup at 11, 5, and 9.

23d.--She took for breakfast an egg and bread-and-butter; and two days later (25th) dinner was added, and also iron.

On the 28th this was the schedule:

On waking, coffee at 7. At 8, iron and malt. Breakfast, a chop, bread-and-butter; of milk, a tumbler and a half. At 11, soup. At 2, iron and malt. Dinner, closing with milk, one or two tumblers. The dinner consisted of anything she liked, and with it she took about six ounces of burgundy or dry champagne. At 4, soup. At 7, malt, iron, bread-and-butter, and usually some fruit, and commonly two glasses of milk. At 9, soup; and at 10 her aloe pill. At 12 M., massage occupied an hour. At 4.30

P.M., electricity was used for an hour in the manner which I have described.

This heavy diet-list, reached in a few days by a woman who had been unable to digest with comfort the lightest meal, seemed certainly surprising. I have not given in full the amount of food eaten at meal-time. Small at first, it was increased rapidly owing to the patient's growing appetite, and became in a few days three large meals.

It is necessary to see the result in one of these successful cases in order to credit it. Mrs. C. began to show gain in flesh about the face in the second week of treatment, and during her two months in bed rose in weight from ninety-six pounds to one hundred and thirty-six; nor was the gain in color less marked.

At the sixth week of treatment the soup was dropped, wine abandoned, the iron lessened one-half, the massage and electricity used on alternate days, and the limbs exercised as I have described. The usual precautions as to rising and exercise were carefully attended to, and at the ninth week of treatment my patient took a drive. At this time all mechanical treatment ceased, the milk was reduced to a quart, the iron to five grains thrice a day, and the malt continued. At the sixth week I began to employ strychnia in doses of one-thirtieth of a grain thrice a day at meals, and this was kept up for several months, together with the iron and malt. The cure was complete and permanent; and its character may be tested by the fact that at the thirtieth day of rest in bed, and after five years of failure to menstruate, to her surprise she had a normal monthly flow. This continued with regularity until eighteen months later, when she became pregnant. The only drawback to her perfect use of all her functions lay in asthenopia, which lasted nearly a year after she left my care. Fatigue of vision for near work is a common condition of the cases I am now describing, and is apt to persist long after all other troubles have vanished. When there is no asthenopia I usually think well of the general chance of recovery; but in no case of feeble vision do I omit at some period of the treatment to have the optical apparatus of the eye looked at with care, because pure asthenopia, apart from all optical defects, is a somewhat rare symptom.

Neither am I always satisfied with the ophthalmologist's dictum that there is a defect so slight as to need no correction, being well aware, as I have elsewhere pointed out, that even minute ocular defects are competent mischief-makers when the brain becomes what I may permit myself, using the photographer's language, to call sensitized by disease.

The following illustrations of success in this mode of treatment are taken from Dr. Playfair's book:[29]

"Early in October of last year I was asked to see a lady thirty-two years of age, with the following history. She had been married at the age of twenty-two, and since the birth of her last child had suffered much from various uterine troubles, described to me by her medical attendant as 'ulceration, perimetritis, and endometritis.' Shortly after the death of her husband, in 1876, these culminated in a pelvic abscess, which opened first through the bladder and afterwards through the vagina. Paralysis of the bladder immediately followed the appearance of pus in the urine, and from that time the urine was never spontaneously voided, and the catheter was always used. Soon after this she began to lose power in the right leg, and then in the left, until they both became completely paralyzed, so that she could not even move her toes, and lay on her back with her legs slightly drawn up, the muscles being much wasted. Towards the end of 1877, after some pain in the back of her neck and twitching of the muscles, she began to lose power in her left arm and in her neck, so that she lay absolutely immobile in bed, the only part of her body she was able to move at all being her right arm. Up to this time the pelvic abscess had continued to discharge through the vagina, and occasionally through the bladder, but it now ceased to do so, and there were no further symptoms referable to the uterine organs. Her general condition, however, remained unaltered, in spite of the most judicious medical treatment. She was seen, from time to time, by several of our most eminent consultants, all of whom recognized the probable hysterical character of her illness, but none of the remedies employed had any beneficial effect. There was almost total anorexia, the amount of food consumed was absurdly small, and the necessary consequence of this inability to take food, combined with four years in bed with paralysis of the greater part of the body, and the habitual use of chloral to induce sleep, had reduced a naturally fine woman to a mere shadow. In October, 1880, her medical attendant was good enough to bring her to London for the purpose of giving a fair trial to the Weir Mitchell method of treatment, with the ready co-operation of herself and her friends, and she was conveyed on a couch slung from the roof of a saloon carriage, so as to avoid any jolt or jar, since the slightest movement caused much suffering. Two days after her arrival my friend Dr.

Buzzard saw her with me, and, after a careful and prolonged electrical examination, came to the conclusion that contractility existed in all the affected muscles, and that the paralysis was purely functional. I could find no evidence in the pelvis of the abscess, the uterus being perfectly mobile, and apparently healthy. After a few days' rest the treatment was commenced on October 16, the patient being isolated in lodgings with a nurse of my own choosing; and this was the only difficulty I had with her, since she naturally felt acutely the separation from the faithful attendant who had nursed her during her long illness. Her friends agreed not to have communication with her of any sort. It is needless to give the details of the treatment in this and the following cases. A mere abstract will suffice to indicate the rapid and satisfactory progress made.

"*October* 16.--Twenty-two ounces of milk were taken, in divided doses, in twenty-four hours; on the 17th, fifty ounces of milk; on the 18th, the same quantity of milk repeated; massage for half an hour; on the 19th, milk as before; bread-and-butter and egg; massage for an hour and a half; twenty minims of dialyzed iron twice daily; on the 21st, a mutton-chop in addition to the above; massage an hour and fifty minutes. To-day she passed water for the first time for four years, and the catheter was never again used. Chloral discontinued, and she slept naturally all night long. On the 23d, porridge and a gill of cream were added to her former diet; massage three hours daily, and electricity for half an hour, and this was continued until the end of the treatment. Maltine was now given twice daily.

"*October* 30.--She is now consuming three full meals daily of fish, meat, vegetables, cream, and fruit, besides two quarts of milk and two glasses of burgundy. Considerable muscular power is returning in her limbs, which she can now move freely in bed.

"*November* 6.--Sat in a chair for an hour. The massage and electricity are being gradually discontinued, and the amount of food lessened.

"*November* 17.--Walked down-stairs, and went out for a drive, and henceforth she went out daily in a Bath-chair. She has increased enormously in size, and looks an entirely different person from the wasted invalid of a few weeks ago.

"On November 26 she went to Brighton quite convalescent, and on December 11 came up of her own accord to see me, drove in a hansom to my house, and returned the same afternoon. She has since remained perfectly strong and well, and has resumed the duties of life and society.

"A somewhat curious phenomenon in this case, which I am unable to account for, was the formation on the anterior surface of the legs, extending from below the patellae half-way down the tibiae, of two large sacs of thin fluid, containing, I should say, each a pint or more, freely fluctuating, and quite painless. I left them alone, and they have spontaneously disappeared."

"In May, 1880, I saw with Dr. Julius, of Hastings, an unmarried lady, aged thirty-one. Her history was that she had been in fairly good health until five years ago, when, during her mother's illness, she overtaxed her strength in nursing, since which time she has been a constant invalid, suffering from backache, bearing down, inability to walk, disordered menstruation, and the usual train of uterine symptoms. She used to get a little better on going to the sea-side, but soon became ill again, and in October, 1879, she was completely laid up. The least standing or walking brought on severe pain in her back and side, and she gave up the attempt, and had since remained entirely confined to her bed or sofa, suffering from constant nausea, complete loss of appetite, and depending on chloral and morphia for relief. Many efforts had been made to break her of this habit, but in vain. Her medical attendant had recognized the existence of a retroflexion, but no pessary remained *in situ* for more than a day or so, and he suspected that she herself pulled them out. I was unable to do more than confirm the diagnosis that had been made as to her local condition, but the pessary I introduced shared the fate of its predecessors, and she remained in the same condition,--in no way benefited by my visit. Things going on from bad to worse, Dr. Julius sent her to London for treatment in the early part of December. I now determined to try the effect of the method I am discussing, of which I knew nothing when I first saw her. It was commenced on December 11, and everything went on most favorably. A week after it was begun, when her attention was fully occupied with the diet, massage, etc., I introduced a stem pessary, being tempted to try this instrument, which I rarely use, by the knowledge that she was at perfect rest, and that no form of Hodge had previously been retained. I do not think she ever knew she had it, and it remained *in situ* for a month, when I removed it and inserted a Hodge, which was thenceforth kept in without any trouble. I may say that I do not think the retroflexion had much to do with her symptoms, except, doubtless, at the commencement of her illness, and she probably would have done quite as well without any local treatment. She rapidly gained flesh and strength, and very soon I entirely stopped both chloral and morphia, and she never seemed to miss them. On December 11, when the treatment was commenced, she weighed 5 st. 9 lbs. On January 20 she weighed 7 st. On January 25 she walked down-stairs, and went out for a drive, and from that time she went out twice daily. She complained of no pain of any kind, and, although she wore a Hodge, she did not seem to have any uterine symptoms. On February 1 she went to the sea-side, looking rosy, fat, and healthy, and has since returned to her home in the country, where she remains perfectly strong and well. A few days ago she came to town, a long railway journey, on purpose to announce to me her approaching marriage."

"On September 10 a gentleman came to consult me on the case of his wife, in consequence of his attention having been directed to my former papers by a relative who is a well-known physician in London. He informed me that his wife was now fifty-five years of age, and that she had passed ten years of her married life in India. At the age of thirty she was much weakened by several successive miscarriages, and then drifted into confirmed ill health. He wrote, on making an appointment, as follows: 'I will give you at once a short outline of her case. We have been married thirty-four years, of which the last twenty have been spent by her in bed or on the sofa. She is unable even to stand, and finds the pain in her back too great to admit of her sitting up. She is utterly without strength, of an intensely nervous temperament, and suffers incessantly from neuralgia. She has, moreover, an outward curvature of the spine. There is not the slightest symptom of paralysis. Fortunately, she does not touch morphia, or any narcotic or stimulant, beyond a glass or two of wine in the day. That she has long been in a state of hysteria is the opinion of nearly all the many medical men who have seen her.'

"Although the attempt to cure so aggravated a case as this was certainly a sufficiently severe test of the treatment, I determined to make the trial, and had the patient removed from her own home and isolated in lodgings. I found her in bed, supported everywhere by many small pillows, and wasted more than, I think, I had ever seen any human being. She really hardly had any covering to her bones, and looked somewhat like the picture of the living skeleton we are familiar with. It may give some idea of her emaciation if I state that, though naturally not a small woman, her height being five feet five and a half inches, she weighed only 4 st. 7 lbs., and

I could easily make my thumb and forefinger meet round the thickest part of the calf of her leg. The curvature of the spine said to exist was a deceptive appearance, produced by her excessive leanness, and the consequent unnatural prominence of the spinous processes of the vertebrae. I could detect no organic disease of any kind. The appetite was entirely wanting, and she consumed hardly any food beyond a little milk, a few mouthfuls of bread, and the like. From the first the patient's improvement was steady and uniform. The way she put on flesh was marvellous, and one could almost see her fatten from day to day. Within ten days all her pains, neuralgia, and backache had gone, and have never been heard of since, and by that time we had also got rid of all her little pillows and other invalid appliances.

"It may be of interest, as showing what this system is capable of, if I copy her food diary on the tenth day after the treatment was begun; and all this, this bedridden patient, who had lived on starvation diet for twenty years, not only consumed with relish, but perfectly assimilated.

"Six A.M.: ten ounces of raw meat soup. 7 A.M.: cup of black coffee. 8 A.M.: a plate of oatmeal porridge, with a gill of cream, a boiled egg, three slices of bread-and-butter, and cocoa. 11 A.M.: ten ounces of milk. 2 P.M.: half a pound of rump-steak, potatoes, cauliflower, a savory omelette, and ten ounces of milk. 4 P.M.: ten ounces of milk and three slices of bread-and-butter. 6 P.M.: a cup of gravy soup. 8 P.M.: a fried sole, roast mutton (three large slices), French beans, potatoes, stewed fruit and cream, and ten ounces of milk. 11 P.M.: ten ounces of raw meat soup.

"The same scale of diet was continued during the whole treatment, and, from first to last, never produced the slightest dyspeptic symptoms, and was consumed with relish and appetite. At the end of six weeks from the day I first saw her she weighed 7 st. 8 lb.,--that is, a gain of 3 st. 1 lb. It will suffice to indicate her improvement if I say that in eight weeks from the commencement of treatment she was dressed, sitting up to meals, able to walk up and down stairs with an arm and a stick, and had also walked in the same way in the park. Considering how completely atrophied her muscles were from twenty years' entire disuse, this was much more than I had ventured to hope. She has now left with her nurse for Natal, and I have no doubt that she will return from her travels with her cure perfected."

"Early in August I was asked to see a lady, aged thirty-seven, with the following history:--'As a girl of sixteen she had a severe neuralgic illness, extending over months: excepting that, she seems to have enjoyed good health until her marriage. Soon after this she had a miscarriage, and then two subsequent pregnancies, accompanied by albuminuria and the birth of dead children.' 'During gestation I was not surprised at all sorts of nervous affections, attributing them to uraemia.' The next pregnancy terminated in the birth of a living daughter, now nearly three years old; during it she had 'curious nervous symptoms,-- *e.g.*, her bed flying away with her, temporary blindness, and vaso-motor disturbances.' Subsequently she had several severe shocks from the death of near relatives, and gradually fell into the condition in which she was when I was consulted. This is difficult to describe, but it was one of confirmed illness of a marked neurotic type. Among other phenomena she had frequently-recurring attacks of fainting. 'These were not attacks of syncope, but of such general derangement of the balance of the circulation that cerebration was interfered with. She was deaf and blind; her face often flushed, sometimes deadly cold; her hands clay-cold, often blue, and difficult to warm with the most vigorous friction. These attacks passed off in from twenty minutes to a couple of hours.' Soon 'the attacks became more frequent, with the reappearance of another old symptom,--acute tenderness of the spine, especially over the sacrum. Then came frequent and persistent attacks of sciatica, and gradual loss of strength.' About this time there appears to have been some uterine lesion, for a well-known gynaecologist went down to the country to see her. Eventually 'she became unable to do anything almost for herself, for the nervous irritability had distressingly increased. To touch her bed, the ringing of a bell, sometimes the sound of a voice, sunlight, &c., affected her so as to make her almost cry out.' 'If she stood up, or even raised her hands to dress her hair, they immediately became blue and deadly cold, and she was done for.' Then followed palpitations of a distressing character, with loud blowing murmur, and pulse of 120 to 140, for which she was seen by an eminent physician, who diagnosed them to be caused by 'slight ventricular asynchronism, with atonic condition of the cardiac as well as of all other muscles of the body.' 'She has no appetite whatever.' 'Any attempt at walking brings on sciatica. She cannot sit, because the tip of the spine is so sensitive; any pressure on it makes her feel faint. She cannot go in a carriage, because it jars every nerve in her body. She cannot lie on her back, because her whole spine is so tender.'

"When consulted about this lady, I gave it as my opinion that any attempt at cure was hopeless as long as she remained in the country house in which she lived. I was informed that it was absolutely impossible to get her away, as she could not bear the motion of any carriage, still less of a railway, without the most acute suffering. Eventually the difficulty was got over by anaesthetizing her, when she was carried on a stretcher to the nearest railway station, and then brought over two hundred miles to London, being all the time more or less completely under the influence of the anaesthetic, administered by her medical attendant, who accompanied her. I found this lady's state fully justified the account given of her. She was intensely sensitive to all sounds and to touch. Merely laying the hand on the bed caused her to shrink, and she could not bear the lightest touch of the fingers on her spine or any part near it. She lay in a darkened room at the back of the house, to be away from the noise of the streets, which distressed her much. She was a naturally fine and highly-cultivated woman, greatly emaciated, with a dusky, sallow complexion, and dark rims round her eyes. I could find no evidence of organic disease of any kind. Whatever lesion of the uterine organs had previously existed had disappeared, and I therefore paid no attention to them. Within a week I had the patient lying in a bright sunlit room in the front of the house, with the windows open, and she complained no longer of the noise. Within ten days the whole spine could be rubbed freely from top to bottom, and from the first I directed the masseuse to be relentless in her manipulation of this part of the body. In a few weeks she had gained flesh largely, the dusky hue of her complexion had vanished, and she looked a different being. The only trouble complained of was sleeplessness, but it did not interfere with the satisfactory progress of the case, and no hypnotic was given. After the first few days we had no return of the nerve-crises which in the country had formed so characteristic a part of her illness. Her hands and feet also, at first of a remarkable deadly coldness, soon became warm, and remained so. In five weeks she was able to sit up, and before the fifth week of treatment was completed I took her out for a drive through the streets in an open carriage for two hours, which she bore without the slightest inconvenience, and the result of which she thus described in a letter the same evening: 'I never enjoyed anything more in my life. I cannot describe my delight and my astonishment at being once more able to drive with comfort. My back has given me no trouble, and I was not really tired.' This lady has since remained perfectly well, and I need give no better proof of this than stating that she has started with her husband on a tour round the world, *via* India, Japan, and San Francisco, and that I have heard from her that she is thoroughly enjoying her travels."

"The last example with which I shall trespass on your patience I am tempted to relate because it is one of the most remarkable instances of the strange and multiform phenomena which neurotic disease may present, which it has ever been my lot to witness. The case must be well known to many members of the profession, since there is scarcely a consultant of eminence in the metropolis who has not seen her during the sixteen years her illness has lasted, besides many of the leading practitioners in the numerous health-resorts she has visited in the vain hope of benefit. My first acquaintance with this case is somewhat curious. About two months before I was introduced to the patient, chancing to be walking along the esplanade at Brighton with a medical friend, my attention was directed to a remarkable party at which every one was looking. The chief personage in it was a lady reclining at full length on a long couch, and being dragged along, looking the picture of misery, emaciated to the last degree, her head drawn back almost in a state of opisthotonos, her hands and arms clenched and contracted, her eyes fixed and staring at the sky. There was something in the whole procession that struck me as being typical of hysteria, and I laughingly remarked, 'I am sure I could cure that case if I could get her into my hands.' All I could learn at the time was that the patient came down to Brighton every autumn, and that my friend had seen her dragged along in the same way for ten or twelve years. On January 14 of this year, I was asked to meet my friend Dr. Behrend in consultation, and at once recognized the patient as the lady whom I had seen at Brighton. It would be tedious to relate all the neurotic symptoms this patient had exhibited since 1864, when she was first attacked with paralysis of the left arm. Among them--and I quote these from the full s furnished by Dr. Behrend--were complete paraplegia, left hemiplegia, complete hysterical amaurosis, but from this she had recovered in 1868. For all these years she had been practically confined to her bed or couch, and had not passed urine spontaneously for sixteen years. Among other symptoms, I find d 'awful suffering in spine, head, and eyes,' requiring the use of chloral and morphia in large doses. 'For many years she has had convulsive attacks of two distinct types, which are obviously of the character of hystero-epilepsy.' The following are the brief s of the condition in which I found her, which I made in my case-book on the day of my first visit. 'I found the patient lying on an invalid couch, her left arm paralyzed and rigidly contracted, strapped to her body to keep it in po- sition. She was groaning loudly at intervals of a few seconds, from severe pain in her back. When I attempted to shake her right hand, she begged me not to touch her, as it would throw her into a convulsion. She is said to have had epilepsy as a child. She has now many times daily, frequently as often as twice in an hour, both during the day and night, attacks of sudden and absolute unconsciousness, from which she recovers with general convulsive movements of the face and body. She had one of these during my visit, and it had all the appearance of an epileptic paroxysm. The left arm and both legs are paralyzed, and devoid of sensation. She takes hardly any food, and is terribly emaciated. She is naturally a clever woman, highly educated, but, of late, her memory and intellectual powers are said to be failing.'

"It was determined that an attempt should be made to cure this case, and she was removed to the Home Hospital in Fitzroy Square. She was so ill, and shrieked and groaned so much, on the first night of her admission, that next day I was told that no one in the house had been able to sleep, and I was informed that it would be impossible for her to remain. Between 3 P.M. and 11.30 P.M. she had had nine violent convulsive paroxysms of an epileptiform character, lasting, on an average, five minutes. At 11.30 she became absolutely unconscious, and remained so until 2.30 A.M., her attendant thinking she was dying. Next day she was quieter, and from that time her progress was steady and uniform. On the fourth day she passed urine spontaneously, and the catheter was never again used. In six weeks she was out driving and walking; and within two months she went on a sea-voyage to the Cape, looking and feeling perfectly well. When there, her nurse, who accompanied her, had a severe illness, through which her ex-patient nursed her most assiduously. She has since remained, and is at this moment, in robust health, joining with plea- sure in society, walking many miles daily, and without a trace of the illnesses which rendered her existence a burden to herself and her friends.

"In conclusion, I may remark that it seems to me that the chief value of this systematic treatment, which is capable of producing such remarkable results, is that it appeals, not to one, but many influences of a curative character. Every one knew, in a vague sort of way, that if an hysterical patient be removed from her morbid surroundings a great step towards cure is made. Few, however, took the trouble to carry this knowledge into practical action; and when they did so they relied on this alone, combined with moral suasion. Now, I am thoroughly convinced that very few cases of hysteria can be preached into health. Judicious moral management can do much; but I believe that very few hysterical women are conscious impostors; and the great efficacy of the Weir Mitchell method seems to me to depend on the combination of agencies which, by restoring to a healthy state a weakened and diseased nervous system, cures the patient in spite of herself."

CHAPTER IX.
DIETETICS AND THERAPEUTICS--(CONTINUED).

As additional illustrations I shall now state a few cases of my own, without entering into minute details of treatment.

The following case is reported by Dr. John Keating, who watched it with care throughout:

P.D., male, aet. 53, after more than thirty years of close attention to business, which severely tried both mental and physical endurance, found himself, in January, 1877, at the close of some months of gradually increasing feebleness, absolutely unable to fulfil his usual duties, and the most alarming symptoms manifested themselves. There was a remarkable loss of nervous and muscular force; his limbs refused their support; his appetite failed; the recollection of ordinary phrases involved distinct and painful effort; sleep became unattainable, except under the influence of powerful narcotics, and even that brief slumber was rendered valueless by the incessant convulsive twitching of the muscles.

His physician prescribed iron and strychnia; ordered an immediate abandonment of all business, and instant departure to a point where telegraph-wires were unknown and mails infrequent. He went at once to the Bahamas, passing a month in that delicious climate in absolute inaction; more than another month was consumed in slowly returning; but, though some flesh had been gained, there was only a trifling improvement in the nervous condition.

May 1, 1877, Dr. Mitchell examined Mr. P.D. The patient was sallow and emaciated, and coughed every few moments. He had night-sweats, nervous twitching, and slight dulness on percussion at the apex of the right lung, with prolonged expiration and roughened inspiration, and some increase of vocal resonance.

Mr. P.D. was allowed to be out of bed once a day four hours, and to spend one hour at his place of business. The treatment was as follows:

At 6 A.M., a tumbler of strong, hot beef-tea, made from the Australian extract.

At 8 A.M., half a tumbler of iron-water, and breakfast, consisting of fruit, steak, potatoes, coffee, and a goblet of milk. At 8.30 A.M., a goblet of milk mixed with a dessertspoonful of Loefland's extract of malt, with six grains of citrate of iron and quinine.

At 10 o'clock Dr. Keating administered the electricity.

At 12 o'clock Mr. P.D. might be dressed, making as little personal effort as possible. The second goblet of milk and malt was administered, and a carriage took him to his office, where he might remain till two o'clock, when the carriage brought him for dinner, preceded by half a tumbler of iron-water. All walking was forbidden.

After dinner (which included a goblet of milk) the third goblet of milk and malt was swallowed; then a short drive might be taken, but by four o'clock the patient must be undressed and in bed.

At 6 P.M. the third dose of iron-water presented itself, and a light supper of fruit, bread-and-butter, and cream, followed by the fourth goblet of milk and malt. Two quarts of milk were thus swallowed every day in addition to all other food.

At 9 P.M., massage one hour, with cocoa-oil, followed by beef-soup, four ounces.

At the fourth week the soup was given up; dialyzed iron was substituted for all other forms. June 4, electricity was given up. The malt was continued until June 20.

May 6, Mr. D. weighed in heavy winter dress one hundred and twenty-five pounds; June 20, in the lightest summer garb, he weighed one hundred and thirty-three pounds; in August his weight rose to one hundred and forty pounds, and he has continued to gain. When last I saw him, a year later, he was strong and well, had no cough, and had ceased to be what he had been for years--a delicate man.

I am indebted to the late Professor Goodell for the following case, which I never saw, but which was carried on with every detail of my treatment. As the testimony of an admirable observer, it is valuable evidence. Professor Goodell writes as follows:

"Some four years ago, Mrs. Y., a very highly intelligent lady, from a neighboring city, came to consult me. She suffered dreadfully at each monthly period, and had constant ovarian pains and a wearying backache, which kept her on a lounge most of the day. She was also barren, and altogether in a pitiable condition. After a two months' treatment she returned home very much better, and soon after conceived. As pregnancy advanced, many of her old symptoms came back, but it was hoped that maternity would rid her of them. The shock of the labor, however, proved too great for her already shattered nervous system. She became far more wretched than before, and again sought my advice.

"At this time I found all her old pains and aches running riot. She got no relief from them night or day without large doses of chloral. The slightest exertion, such as sewing, writing, and reading for a few minutes, greatly wearied her. Even the simple mental effort of casting up the weekly housekeeping expenses of a very small household upset her, and she had to give it up. The act of walking one of our blocks, or of going down a short flight of stairs, or of riding for an hour in a well-padded carriage, gave her such 'unspeakable agony'--to use her own words--that she would have an hysterical attack of screams and tears. So emotional had this constant nerve-strain made her that she could not sustain an ordinary conversation without giving way to tears. Much of her time was spent in bed; in fact, she was practically bedridden.

"I tried in vain to wean her from her anodynes, and failed altogether in doing her any good, although many remedies were resorted to, and various modes of treatment adopted. Finally, in sheer despair, I put her to bed, and began your treatment of rest, with electricity, massage, and frequent feeding. The first trace of improvement showed itself in a greater self-control, and in a lessening of her aches and pains. Next, smaller doses of the anodyne were needed, until it was wholly withheld. Then she began to pick up an appetite, which, towards the close of the treatment, became so keen that, between three good meals every day, she drank several goblets of milk and of beef-tea. At the outset I had stipulated for six weeks of this treatment, and it was with reluctance that my patient yielded to my wish. But when the time was up she had become so impressed with the wonderful benefits she had received and was receiving, that she begged to have the treatment continued for two weeks more. At the end of that time she had gained at least thirty pounds in weight, and had lost every pain and ache. Her night-terrors, which I forgot to mention as one of her distressing symptoms, had wholly disappeared, and she could sleep from nine to ten hours at a stretch. I now sent her into the country, where she is continuing to mend, and is astonishing her friends by her scrambles up and down the steep hills.

"Such were the salient features of this case; and I can assure you that I was as much impressed by the happy results of the treatment as were a host of anxious and doubting friends.

"Very faithfully yours, "WM. GOODELL."

*   *   *   *   *

Miss C., an interesting woman, aet. 26, at the age of 20 passed through a grave trial in the shape of nursing her mother through a typhoid fever. Soon after, a series of calamities deprived her of fortune, and she became, for support, a clerk, and did for two years eight hours' work daily. Under these successive strains her naturally sturdy health gave way. First came pain in the back, then growing paleness, loss of flesh, and unending sense of tire. Her work, which was a necessity, was of course kept up, steadily at first, but was soon interfered with by increase of the menstrual flow, with unusual pain and persistent ovarian tenderness. Very soon she began to drop her work for a day at a time. Then came an increasing asthenopia, with evening headaches, until her temper changed and became capricious and irritable. When I saw her, she had been forced to abandon all labor, and had been treated by an accomplished gynaecologist, and was said to be cured of a prolapsus uteri and of extensive ulceration, despite which relief she gained nothing in vigor and endurance and got back neither color nor flesh.

She went to bed December 10, and rose for the first time February 4, having gained twenty-nine pounds. She went to bed pale, and got up actually ruddy. In a month she returned to her work again, and has remained ever since in health which enables her, as she writes me, "to enjoy work, and to do with myself what I like."

Miss L., aet. 26, came to me with the following history. At the age of 20 she had a fall, and began in a week or two to have an irritable spine. Then, after a few months, a physician advised rest, to which she took only too kindly, and in a year from the time of her accident she was rarely out of bed. Surrounded by highly sympathetic relatives, to whom chronic illness was somewhat novel, she speedily developed, with their tender aid, hyperaesthetic states of the eye and ear, so that her nurses crept about in a darkened room, the piano was silenced, and the children kept quiet. By slow degrees a whole household passed under the selfish despotism of an hysterical girl. Intense constipation, anorexia, and alternate states of dysuria, anuria, and polyuria followed, and before long her sister began to fail in health, owing to the incessant exactions to which she too willingly yielded. This alarmed a brother, who insisted upon a change of treatment, and after some months she was brought on a couch to this city.

At the time I first saw her, she took thirty grains of chloral every night and three hypodermic injections of one-half grain of morphia daily. As to food, she took next to none, and I could only guess her weight at about ninety pounds. She was in height five feet two and a half inches, and very sallow, with pale lips, and the large, indented tongue of anaemia. I made the most careful search for signs of organic mischief, and, finding none, I began my treatment as usual with milk, and added massage and electricity without waiting. Her digestion seemed so good that I gave lactate of iron in twenty-grain doses from the third day, and also the aloes pill thrice a day. It is perhaps needless to state that I isolated her with a nurse she had never seen before, and that for seven weeks she saw no one else save myself and the attendants. The full schedule of diet was reached at the end of a fortnight, but the chloral and morphia were given up at the second day. She slept well the fourth night, and, save that she had twice a slight return of polyuria, went on without a single drawback. In two months she was afoot and weighed one hundred and twenty-one pounds. Her change in tint, flesh, and expression was so remarkable that the process of repair might well have been called a renewal of life.

She went home changed no less morally than physically, and resumed her place in the family circle and in social life, a healthy and well-cured woman.

I might multiply these histories almost endlessly. In some cases I have cured without fattening; in others, though rarely, the mental habits formed through years of illness have been too deeply ingrained for change, and I have seen the patient get up fat and well only to relapse on some slight occasion.

The intense persistency with which some women study and dwell upon their symptoms is often the great difficulty. Even a slight physical annoyance becomes for one of these unhappily-constituted natures a grave and almost ineradicable trouble, owing to the habit of self-study.

Miss P., aet. 29, weight one hundred and eleven pounds, height five feet four inches, dark-skinned, sallow, and covered with the acne of bromidism, had had one attack which was considered to have been epileptic, and which was probably hysterical, but on this matter she dwelt with incessant terror, which was fostered by the tender care of a near relative, who left her neither by night nor by day. Vague neuralgic aches in the limbs, with constant weariness, asthenopia, anaemia, loss of appetite, and loss of flesh, followed. Then came spinal pain and irregular menstruation, a long course of local cauterizations of the womb, spinal braces, and endless tonics and narcotics.

I broke up the association which had nearly been fatal to both women, and, confidently promising a cure, carried out my treatment in full In three months she went home well and happy, greatly improved in looks, her skin clear, her functions regular, and weighing one hundred and thirty-six pounds.

It is vain to repeat the relation of such cases, and impossible to put on paper the means for deciding--what is so large a part of success in treatment--the moral methods of obtaining confidence and insuring a childlike acquiescence in every needed measure.

Another class of cases will, however, bear some further illustration. We meet with women who are healthy in mind, but who have some chronic pain or some definite malady which does not get well, either because the usual tonics fail, or because their occupations in life keep them always in a state of exhaustion. If by rest we slow the machinery, and by massage and electricity deprive rest of its evils, we can often obtain cures which are to be had in no other way. This is true of many uterine and of some other disorders.

Miss B., aet. 37, height five feet five inches, weight one hundred and fifteen pounds, a schoolteacher, without any notable organic disease, had a severe fall, owing to an accident while driving. A slight swelling in the hurt lumbar region was followed by pain, which became intense when she walked any distance. Loss of color, flesh, and appetite ensued, and, after much treatment, she consulted me. I could find nothing beyond soreness on deep pressure, and she was anything but hysterical or emotional.

Two months' rest with the usual treatment brought her weight up to one hundred and thirty-eight pounds, and she has been able ever since to do her usual work, and to walk when and where and as far as she wished.

Several years ago I treated with some reluctance a lady who had extensive bronchitis and a slight albuminuria. This woman was a mere skeleton, with every function out of order. I undertook her case with the utmost distrust, but I had the pleasure to find her fattening and reddening like others. Her cough left her, the albumen disappeared, and she became well enough to walk and drive; when a sudden congestion of the kidneys destroyed her in forty-eight hours.

The following case of extreme anaemia, with striking resemblance to the pernicious type in some of its features, is especially interesting for the ease and rapidity of improvement under rest and massage without electricity or excessive amounts of food.

Mrs. T., aet. 40, the mother of several children, had been unwell for years, and almost totally incapacitated for exertion for two years before admission, in January, 1894. She complained of extreme feebleness, distaste for and inability to digest food, a great and constant difficulty in swallowing, shortness of breath, dropsy of the ankles if she walked or stood, hemorrhoids from which some bleeding often occurred, extreme constipation, constant chilliness, and frequent violent headaches. Her appearance was that of a person with pernicious anaemia, a very yellow muddy skin, dry and harsh to the touch, and the hands and feet cold, almost to the point of pain.

On examination the spleen was decidedly large; the lower border of the stomach reached to the level of the umbilicus. Two cardiac murmurs were present, the one a sharp and well-defined mitral regurgitant sound, confirmed by the dyspnoea and dropsy as organic, the other a loud musical murmur of haemic origin. The trouble in deglutition proved to be due to an oesophageal narrowing. The blood examination bore out the suggestion of probable pernicious anaemia, the red cells being only 1,500,000, haemoglobin 18 per cent.: the microscope showed microcytes, megaloblasts, nucleated red cells, and a large increase in white corpuscles. In order to study the effect of massage alone upon the blood no other treatment was used, though of course the patient was kept at "absolute rest." No drugs were given, electricity was not used, and extra food was omitted, as the irritability of the oesophagus made her unwilling to attempt the exertion and annoyance of frequent feeding. The general chilliness was at once helped by massage, and in a few days only felt in the small hours of the night, and the patient gained weight from the first. After one week of treatment a blood count was made: red cells were 3,800,000, more than double the former figure; haemoglobin, 35 per cent., almost double its original value. On the same day, one hour after the completion of an hour's massage, the corpuscular count had attained 5,400,000, the haemoglobin remaining 35 per cent.

At the end of two weeks the haemic murmur had faded into a faint soft bruit, though the mitral murmur was unchanged, the skin had improved in color, the aches and weariness were gone, and the blood count had reached nearly five million cells, with 50 per cent. of haemoglobin. The extraordinary results of the blood examination were confirmed by observations made by Professor Frederick P. Henry, Dr. Judson Daland, and Dr. J.K. Mitchell, who all practically agreed. Professor Henry made several studies and stained a number of slides, verifying in his report the statements of the presence of megaloblasts and nucleated red cells made above.

Owing to the necessity for an operation on the hemorrhoids, which caused loss of blood, the patient was somewhat retarded in her progress to recovery, but by the tenth week was so far better that the blood showed no microscopic abnormalities, the count was full normal, and the haemoglobin over 70 per cent. Her color and strength were good, the heart was perfectly strong, the anaemic murmur was gone, and the oesophagus was so much less irritable that it was possible to begin dilatation of the stricture.

I have heard within a year that though occasionally annoyed by this last trouble if she becomes much fatigued, she has remained in other ways well.

Mrs. G., the daughter of nervous parents, was always a nervous, over-sensitive, serious child, worked hard at Vassar, broke down, recovered, returned to college, was attacked with measles, which proved severe, and by the time she graduated had been made by her own tendencies and the anxious attention of her family into a devoted member of the class which I may permit myself to describe as health-maniacs.

Health-foods, health-corsets, health-boots, the deeply serious consideration of how to eat, on which side to sleep, profound examination of whether mutton or lamb were the more digestible flesh,--these were her occupations,--and two or three years before her panic about her health had been made worse by the discovery of an aortic stenosis, of which an over-frank doctor had thought it best to inform her. When I saw her she had been three years married, was childless, and, between the real cardiac disease and her own anxieties about it, had driven herself into a state of great physical debility and a mental condition approaching delusional insanity.

A too restricted diet, lacking both in variety and appetizingness, had had its usual result of upsetting digestion and destroying desire for food. Even with the small amounts which she ate she considered it necessary to chew so carefully and to feed herself so slowly that from one hour to an hour and a half was used for each meal. The heart, under-nourished, beat feebly, there was constant slight albuminuria with evidences of congested kidneys, and she could only rest in a semi-erect position.

The heart condition, with its renal results, proved the most rebellious part of the trouble. A firm and intelligent nurse soon overcame the difficulties and delays about food, and my final refusal to discuss them disposed for the time of some of the fanciful theories about digestion and so on. Her meals were ordered in every detail, and she was told that they were prescribed and to be taken like medicine, and, fed by the nurse, she began to take more nourishment. Massage relieved some of the labor of the heart, and gradually the semi-erect posture was exchanged inch by inch for a semi-recumbent one. Not to prolong the relation of details, it was found needful to keep this lady in bed for five months before the heart seemed to recover sufficiently to allow her to get up. Even then, although improved in color, flesh, and blood condition, she had to attain an erect station almost as slowly as she had had to reach recumbency. Slow, active Swedish movements, to which gentle resistance movements were very gradually added, helped the heart. Her cure was completed by five or six months' camp-life in the woods, and she is now the mother of a healthy child and herself perfectly well, the valvular disease only to be detected by the most careful examination, and never, even during pregnancy and parturition, causing any annoyance.

The surgeons, who once thought a floating kidney could be permanently fixed in its place by stitching, have now concluded that this is very doubtful, and the treatment of this displacement is never very satisfactory by any method. Still, some success has followed long rest in the supine position, which encourages the kidney to return to its normal place, until careful full feeding has renewed or increased the fatty cushions which hold it up. It is best during the first weeks of treatment not to allow the patient to sit or stand, or if she should be unable to avoid the occasional need for these positions, an abdominal binder must be applied by the nurse and drawn tightly before she moves. The masseuse is directed to avoid any movements which might further displace the organ, and may cautiously push it upward and hold it there with one hand while with the other the manipulation of the abdomen is performed. However long it may require, the patient should not get up until examinations, supine, lateral, prone, and erect, combine to assure us that the kidney is replaced. Repeated investigation of this point will be required,--for the kidney will sometimes be in place for a little while and next day or even a few hours later have slipped down again. Before any exertion is permitted, even ordinary walking, an accurate close-fitting abdominal belt with a kidney-pad should be applied. Those kept in stock are seldom properly adjusted, and usually have the pad in the wrong place. If rightly made, they can be worn with comfort and tight enough to be useful. If not rightly made, they are useless instruments of torture.

Mrs. Y., aet. fifty-six, was sent to Dr. J.K. Mitchell by Professor Osler for treatment. She had all the usual intestinal derangements and discomforts attendant upon a floating kidney: constipation alternated with diarrhoea, or rather with a sort of intestinal incontinence; vague pains in the back, flanks, and stomach were frequent; attacks of acute pain began in the right hypogastrium and ran down to the symphysis or into the groin; she had constant flatulence, weight, and oppression after food; was pale, flabby, and emaciated, but had no emotional or nervous symptoms except an annoying amount of insomnia. The lower border of the stomach was fully two inches below the navel in the middle-line, even when only a glass of water had been taken. It was a little lower after a small meal. The colon was distended and very variable in position, probably changing its relations with the landmarks as it happened to be more or less filled with food or gases. The abdominal walls were flabby, relaxed, and pendulous, and the whole surface tender. The patient gave a history of sudden loss of flesh with almost no reason some three years before, and increasing indigestion in all forms ever since. The tenderness made careful abdominal study difficult, but lessened enough after a few days in bed to permit the perception of a displacement of the right kidney, whose lower edge could be felt on a level with the umbilicus and two inches to the right of it. No change of position would bring it any lower. Examined with the patient prone, two-thirds of the kidney could be outlined, extremely tender, and causing nausea and sinking if pressed upon.

The chief trouble in treatment proved to be the irritability of the intestines, which was brought on in most unexpected fashion by foods of the simplest kind. For some time it was so persistent that the suspicion of intestinal tuberculosis was entertained; but it finally disappeared, and after that the case progressed more favorably and she was out of bed with a tight belt and kidney-pad in a little more than twelve weeks. The kidney was then, and has remained since, in its normal position. The patient gained twelve pounds in weight, and should have gained more, but she found the hot weather during the latter weeks of her treatment very trying. The intestinal indigestion was only partially relieved, but the gastric symptoms, the general pains, and weakness all disappeared, and with precaution she will continue to improve. It is best to advise the constant use of the belt in such a case. In a patient who has made a large gain in flesh, as this one did not, and who has been found after some months to maintain the increased weight, the belt might gradually and experimentally be left off; but repeated examinations should be made for a year or two to be sure that no displacement results.

I could relate cases of gain in flesh without manifest relief. As I have said, these are rare; but it is less uncommon to see great relief without improvement in weight at all, or until the patient is up and afoot for some weeks; and I could also state several cases in which a repetition of the treatment won a final and complete success after the first effort at cure had failed or but partially succeeded; and of this, I believe, Professor Goodell has seen several examples.

I have mentioned more than once the singular return of menstruation under this treatment, and as examples I add a brief list of some notable instances.

Mrs. N., aet. 29, no menstruation for five years; return of menstruation at thirtieth day of treatment; continued regularly ever since during three years.

Mrs. C., aet. 42, eight years without menstruation; return at fourteenth day of treatment; now regular during five months.

Miss C., aet. 22, no menstruation for eight months; return at close of sixtieth day of treatment; regular now for four months.

Miss A., aet. 26, irregular; missing for two or three months, and then menstru-ating irregularly for two or three months. No flow for two months. Menstruated at nineteenth day of treatment, and regular during thirteen months ever since.

I had at one time intended to give, in the first edition of this work, a summary of all my cases, with the results; but what is easy to do in definite maladies like ty-phoid fever becomes hard in cases such as I here relate. In fevers the statistics are simple,--patients die or get well; but in cases of nervous exhaustion, so called, it is impossible to state accurately the number of partial recoveries, or, at least, to define usefully the degrees of gain. For these reasons I have not attempted to furnish full statistics of the large number of cases I have treated.

In the debate before the British Medical Association the question of the per-manence of cures by this method was the subject of discussion. I have lately been at some pains to learn the fate of many of my earlier cases, and can say with certainty that every case then treated was selected because all else had failed, and that I find relapses into the state they were in when brought to me to have been very uncom-mon. A vast proportion have remained in useful health, and a small number have lost a part of their gains. I now make it a rule to keep up some relation with patients after discharge, by occasional visits or by letter, and believe that in this way many small troubles are hindered from becoming large enough to cause relapses.

I said in my first edition that I did not doubt that the statements I made would give rise in some minds to that distrust which the relation of remarkable cures so naturally excites; and this I cannot blame. Every physician can recall in his own practice such cases as I have described, and every medical man of large experience knows that many of these women are to him sources of anxiety or of therapeutic despair so deep that after a time he gets to think of them as destined irredeemably to a life of imperfect health, and finds it hard to believe that any method of treatment can possibly achieve a rescue.

I am fortunate now in having been able to show that in other hands than my own, both here and abroad, this treatment has so thoroughly justified itself as to need no further defence or apology from its author. It has gratified me also to learn that in many instances country physicians, remote from the resources of great cit-ies, have been able to make it available. As I have already said, I am now more fear-ful that it will be misused, or used where it is not needed, than that it will not be used; and, with this word of caution, I leave it again to the judgment of time and my profession.

CHAPTER X.
THE TREATMENT OF LOCOMOTOR ATAXIA, ATAXIC PARAPLEGIA, SPASTIC PARALYSIS, AND PARALYSIS AGITANS.

In my earliest publication on the treatment of diseases by rest, etc., locomotor ataxia was alluded to as one of the troubles in which remarkable results had been obtained. Rest alone will do much to diminish pain and promote sleep in tabes, rest with massage and electricity will do more. It is not necessary to order complete seclusion for such cases, but some special measures will be needed in addition to those already described as of use in various disorders, and these will be discussed in this chapter.

While this is not a treatise on diagnosis, some brief symptom-description is needed to enable one to define clearly the methods of treatment at different stages.

In the middle or late stages there need be little uncertainty in uncomplicated cases; in the earlier periods diagnosis is by no means easy. A history may usually be elicited of important heralding symptoms, such as former or present troubles with the muscles of the eyes, the occurrence of vague but sharp and recurring pains, vertigo, an impairment of balance, unnoticed perhaps, except when walking in the dark or when stooping to wash the face, or especially when going down stairs. Attacks of 'dyspepsia,' as unrecognized visceral crises are often called, should render one suspicious. If, on examination, loss or impairment of knee-jerk be shown, contraction of the pupil with Argyll-Robertson phenomenon and defective station, but little doubt can exist. The discovery by the ophthalmoscope of some degree of beginning optic neuritis would make assurance more sure, and this can often be detected in a very early stage of the disease.

Much controversy has been spent on the question of the share of syphilis in producing tabes, and out of the battle but two facts emerge fairly certain, the one that syphilis often precedes the disease, the other that anti-syphilitic medication is commonly of no service. But syphilis is so frequently antecedent that a history of that infection may make certain the diagnosis when doubt exists. This may be an important point, for some of the cardinal symptoms are occasionally absent; cases are seen with no incooerdination, sometimes with the station unaffected, even, though rarely, with the knee-jerk preserved.

The diagnosis established, treatment will somewhat depend upon the stage which the disease has reached.

In the pre-ataxic stage, where slight unsteadiness, often not troublesome except in the dark or with closed eyes, sharp stabbing pains here and there, numbness of the feet, girdle-sense in the region of chest, waist, or belly, some recurrent difficulty in emptying the bladder, a fugitive partial palsy of the external muscles of the eye, are the chief or, perhaps, the only complaints, it would not be justifiable to put the patient to bed at complete rest. This early stage calls for a different plan of treatment, to be presently described.

In the middle or more distinctly ataxic period long rest in bed should be prescribed, and will be gratefully accepted by a patient whose sufferings from incooerdination, pains, and numbness of the extremities are often so great as to incapacitate him.

The bladder muscles share in the ataxia, and the consequent retention of urine frequently causes cystitis, and may endanger life by the involvement of the kidneys.

The bowels cannot be emptied or are moved without the patient's knowledge, and these annoyances combine with the pain and nervous apprehension to drive the victim into a melancholic or neurasthenic state. He suffers, too, from want of occupation, from the absence of exercise, from the anticipation of worse changes in the near future, and usually by the time he reaches the specialist has been more or less poisoned with iodide of potash and mercury, and perhaps with morphia.

In the third, the paralytic stage, which seldom comes on until the symptoms have lasted for years, there is gradual loss of power and ataxia, increasing until he is totally unable to walk. If a patient is not seen until this condition of things has been reached, but little can be hoped from any treatment, though in a few cases energetic measures may bring about a marked improvement, which is rarely lasting.

A combination of tabes with lateral sclerosis, or with general paralysis of the insane, is sometimes seen, but needs no special consideration.

The first or pre-ataxic stage is, to the great detriment of patients, too seldom recognized. The pains are called rheumatic, the eye symptoms are lightly passed over or glasses are ordered, the difficulty of micturition is treated by drugs, and the slightly impaired balance unnoticed or unconsidered.

When such a patient comes into our hands the history, and especially the history of predisposing causes, needs the most careful examination. It is well established that syphilis is a common precedent of ataxia, occurring in at least two-thirds of the cases; it is even more firmly settled that iodide and mercury in large doses do no good in advanced ataxia. I say in advanced ataxia, because a few cases are seen in which the syphilis has been of recent occurrence, or where the spinal symptoms are of decidedly acute character, and in these anti-syphilitic medication is needed and useful; but such cases should be described as acute or subacute spinal syphilis, not as ataxia. When nerve degeneration has once begun, iodide will do little good and mercury may do positive harm, if used in large doses. The other common predisposing causes, exposure to cold, over-exertion, sexual excess, need concern us only as they suggest warnings to be given, especially when the patient is improving. Until he does improve not much need be said about them; he cannot indulge in venery, as sexual power is usually (though not always) lost early in the disease; and the incoöerdination lessens his opportunities of exposure or over-exertion.

During this stage some patients complain most of the numbness, girdle-sense, and incoöerdination; others of the stabbing pains or the bladder weakness. The general treatment must be much the same, however, in all, with special attention besides to the special needs of each individual.

Fatigue makes all the symptoms worse, increases pain, and impairs still more the muscular incoöerdination; it is, therefore, of the first importance in every instance to forbid all over-exertion. Walking, more than any other form of exercise, hurts these cases. The patient should not walk beyond his absolute necessities. To get the needed fresh air, let him, according to his situation in life, drive out or use the street-cars. In some cases the use of a tricycle on a level floor or on good roads is not so harmful as walking, for obvious reasons; this tricycle exercise may at first be made a passive or mild exercise by having the machine pushed by an attendant. To replace the effects upon the circulation and bowels of physical activity massage may be used, and the masseur must have directions as to gentle handling of the tender places at first. These are usually in fixed positions, and can be avoided or only lightly touched. The shooting pains may be lessened by deep, slow massage in the tracks of the nerves affected. If, as generally happens, there are also regions of defective sensation, these should receive after the general manipulation active, rapid circular friction, and, perhaps, experimentally, open-hand slapping. As constipation is one of the troublesome features, the abdomen should have particular attention, and an unusual amount of time be given to manipulations of the colon, as described in the chapter on massage. A full hour's rest in bed, preferably in a darkened room, must follow the rubbing.

A schedule for the day on about the lines of the "partial rest" schedule, as described on a previous page, should be followed. A prolonged warm bath, with cool sponging after, if the latter be well borne, is useful in lessening pains and nervous irritability,--and this may begin the day or be used at any convenient hour.

At an hour as far from the massage as possible lessons in co-ordinate movements are given, after a week or ten days of massage has prepared the muscles, and baths and a quiet life have steadied the nerves. For many years past, certainly fifteen or sixteen, the students and physicians who have followed my service at the Infirmary for Nervous Diseases have seen this systematic training given, and no doubt they received with some amusement the excitement about it as a new method of treatment when it was proclaimed in Europe two or three years ago.

The indication for this teaching appeared too obvious to publish or talk much about. The patient has incooerdination; one, therefore, does one's best to teach him to co-ordinate his movements by small beginnings and by small increases.

The lessons may be given by the physician at first and be executed under his eye. After a few days any tolerably intelligent patient should be able to carry them out alone, but still each new movement should be personally inspected to make sure that it is done correctly.

In patients in the first stage of ataxia the most striking result of incooerdination is the impairment of station. We therefore begin with balancing lessons. The patient is directed to stand at "Attention," head up and chest out, not looking at his feet, as the ataxic always wishes to do. At first this is enough to require; it will not do to be too particular about how his feet are placed, so long as he does not straddle. He can repeat this effort for himself a dozen times a day, for a minute or two each time. Next we try the same position with a little more care about getting the feet pretty near together and parallel, or with the toes turned out only a very little. In another couple of days a little more severity may be exercised about maintaining the correct attitude,--heels touching, hands hanging down, and eyes looking straight forward,--and until he is able to do this *easily* it is best to ask nothing more. Then he is requested to stand on one foot, being permitted just to touch a chair-back or the attendant's hand to give confidence. This is practised until he can keep his erect station for a few seconds without difficulty. This point of improvement may be reached in three days or a week or may take a fortnight. Women, as I have before observed, although rarely in America the victims of tabes, when they do have it have far less disturbance of balance than men, and this is to be attributed to their life-long habit of walking without seeing their feet. I have found in the few cases of ataxia in women that I have seen that they benefited much more quickly by these balance instructions than did men, though their other symptoms were in no way different.

Continuing every day the practice of all the previous lessons, movements are rapidly added as soon as station is better. A brief list of them follows. When the exercises grow so numerous as to take overmuch time, the simpler early ones may be omitted.

When the learner is able to stand on one foot, let him slowly raise the other and put it on a marked spot on the edge of a chair. This, like all the other exercises, must be practised with both feet.

Stand erect without bending forward and put one foot straight back as far as possible.

Do the same sideways.

Stand and bend body slowly forward, backward, and sideways, with a moment's rest after each motion.

Having reached this point, I usually order the patient to practise all these with closed eyes. When he can do this, he begins to take one or two steps with shut eyes, first forward, then sideways, then backward. If he falter or move without freedom, he is kept at this until he does it confidently. Then exercises in following patterns traced on the floor are begun. In hospitals, or where bare floors are to be found, the patterns may be drawn with chalk. In carpeted rooms, which by the way are less suited for the work than plain boards or parquet floors, a piece of half-inch wide white tape may be laid in the required pattern, first in a straight line, later, as proficiency is gained, in curved, figure-of-eight, or angular patterns. The patient must be made to walk *on* the line, putting one foot directly in front of the other, with the heel of the forward foot touching the toe of the one behind.

Walking over obstacles is tried next. Wooden blocks measuring about six by twelve inches and two inches thick are stood on edge at intervals of eighteen inches and the patient walks over them, thus training several groups of muscles; the blocks are at first set in straight lines, then in curving patterns. An ordinary octavo book makes a good substitute for a block.

If the trunk muscles are affected by the ataxia, further exercises are ordered for them, bending and twisting movements, picking up objects from the floor, etc. For the hands and arms, which, except in those very rare cases where the ataxia first shows itself in the upper extremities, seldom exhibit much incooerdination in the primary and middle stages, the movements are the picking up of a series of different-shaped small articles, arranging objects like dominoes, marbles, or the kindergarten sticks in patterns, bringing the fingers of the two hands one after another together, or touching a finger to the ear or the nose, at first with open and then with shut eyes.

With these methods, needing not more than twenty minutes three times a day, the ataxic symptoms sometimes rapidly diminish. In certain cases no other improvement will be observed, showing that what has taken place is of course not an alteration of the diseased nerve-tissues for the better, as no treatment can restore sclerotic spinal tissue to a normal state, but is merely a substitution of function, in which other and associated nerve-tracts have replaced in control the ones affected.

As to the pains and bowel and bladder disturbances, their handling will be discussed in considering the treatment of the next or middle stage of tabes. In this period the ataxic symptoms are most prominent; the gait has become so unsteady that the patient needs canes to walk at all and must constantly watch his feet. He walks a little better when well under way, but at starting or when standing still he sways and totters. The girdle-sense is severe and constant, various pains assail the body and limbs; the numbness of the feet, often described as a feeling "like walking with a pillow under the foot," still further incommodes his walking.[30] The bladder control may be so enfeebled as to require daily catheterization, and the bowels move only with enemas or purgatives, and often without the patient's knowledge, owing to the anaesthesia which affects the rectum and its vicinity.

One of the first things to attend to when patients are in this stage is the bladder, as the retention is the only condition likely to produce serious disorder. Cystitis is or may be present, and with the retention is a constant threat to the kidneys. Catheterization and washing out with an antiseptic must be regularly practised while treatment is used to improve the condition.

For these patients rest in bed is a prime necessity in order to remove all excuse for exertion. The method of application of massage has already been suggested. Care must be taken that the patient eats well and of the best food. Except for occasional gastric or intestinal crises of pain, sometimes with vomiting, sometimes with diarrhoea, the digestive functions are usually well performed, unless the stomach has been greatly upset by over-use of iodide. The most liberal feeding consistent with good digestion is indicated, for it must be remembered that we are dealing with a disease in which degenerative changes play an important part. The usefulness of electricity in ataxia has been denied by some authors, while others praise it indiscriminately. Perhaps a reason for this difference of opinion may be found in its different effects upon individual patients; but I see few in whom I do not find electricity in one or another form helpful. For pains I order the galvanic current through the affected nerves as strong as the man is able to bear. If after a few days of this the pains are unchanged, a rapidly interrupted faradic current is tried, and failing to do good with this, I use light cauterization or a series of small blisters to the spine at the point of exit of the painful nerves. Galvanization of the bladder with an intravesical electrode is sometimes of service to strengthen its capacity for contraction. Faradism is applied in the form just described, using a wire brush as an electrode to the areas of numbness and anaesthesia. Lately I have found that this current in a strength which would be very painful to the normal skin will in some instances relieve the feeling of pressure and dull discomfort about the rectum and perineum, and it has been successful when galvanism did no good. In patients within reach of a static machine, this form may be used for the numbness if the others do not help it.

For the attacks of pain, if general, a prolonged hot bath lasting from ten to twelve minutes, at a temperature of 100 deg. F. or even more, should be first tried; if this fail, antipyrin, phenacetin, acetanilid, or cannabis indica may be used, or, as a last resort, morphia. For the local pains hot water is also useful, and in the intervals I order applications of hot water to the tender points, as hot as can be borne, alternating with ice-water, each rapidly applied three or four times. In severe attacks, and with all due caution to avoid habituation, cocaine injections may be given. In cases with high arterial tension the daily administration of nitroglycerin in full doses will not only lower the tension but decrease the pains in force and frequency.

For several years past in all patients with the general lowering of nervous force and vitality so common in this disease I have habitually used the testicular elixir of Brown-Sequard. The ridiculous length to which organic therapeutics have been carried, the extravagant advertising claims, and an absurd expectation of impossible results have combined to make the profession shy of those organic preparations which have not very good evidence in their favor, and for some time I shared in this prejudice against the Brown-Sequard fluid. A talk with that most distinguished physician and an examination of some of his cases led me to a trial for myself, and I am at present very well convinced that, whether a physiologic basis can reasonably be assumed or not, we have in the fluid a tonic remedy of great power. While I have used it with good effect in other conditions, it is in ataxia that I have found it of most value.

The glycerin extract is freshly prepared from bulls' testicles in exact accordance with the directions of the discoverer. It is used hypodermatically every other day, beginning with a diluted ten-minim dose and increasing by two or three drops up to about forty minims. The effect is at its height twelve to twenty-four hours after the administration in most patients, hence the reason for using it only once in two days. The skin is prepared, the needles and syringe disinfected, and the tiny puncture sealed afterwards with as minute care as would be given to a surgical operation.

By these precautions the danger of abscess, always considerable if hypodermics are carelessly given, is minimized. As the dose is large, a site must be selected for the injection where the tissue is loose, otherwise the pain will interfere with the desired frequency of use. The buttocks serve best, or the outer masses of the pectoral muscles, or the abdominal muscles. If the administration causes pain (due in part to the large quantity used and in part to the local effect of glycerin), a fraction of a grain of cocaine may be added to the solution when measured out for use.

It may at once be said, emphatically, that in some cases remarkable results have followed the use of this material, while in others no good has been done; but the same may be said of most plans of treatment in this disorder. As to possible danger from it, no harm has been done to any patient known to me, except that abcesses have occurred sometimes, though very rarely, for in many hundreds of injections it has been my good fortune to see abscesses form only three or four times, two of these instances, by curious ill luck, being in physicians. Patients describe a stimulating effect not unlike that of strong coffee, following a few hours after use and lasting for a day. The sexual appetite, if present, is increased; if absent, it is often renewed, sometimes in elderly men to an inconvenient extent. In one tabetic subject who had lost desire and ability for more than three years both returned in sufficient force to allow him to beget a child. This patient, like most of the others, was ignorant of what drug was being used and of what effects might be expected, so suggestion played no part. Apart from this special effect, the solution acts only as a highly stimulating tonic.

The full dose of forty minims or thereabouts is maintained for a fortnight or less, and then gradually diminished in the same way that it was increased. Sometimes, when the effect has been good, a second "course" may be given after two or three weeks' interval.

During the treatment by hypodermic the masseur should be told to avoid rubbing where the injections have been given. A few trials with the fluid internally have produced so little result of any kind that I am inclined to think the gastric juices must alter it so as to lessen or wholly destroy its power.

As to other drugs, experience has not given me much confidence in any of those usually recommended. Strychnia, belladonna, and those antiseptic drugs which are eliminated chiefly by the kidneys are of use when cystitis has to be treated and the bladder muscles urged to activity. Arsenic, the chloride of gold and sodium, and chloride of aluminium are suggested by various authorities, but they have not been of any value in my hands. In hopeless cases, where all treatment fails, as will sometimes happen, or in patients in whom the paralytic stage is already far advanced, if other measures are unsuccessful, morphia is left as a forlorn hope, which will at least relieve their pains.

An outline report of several cases of different types and degrees is appended:

M.P. of North Carolina, aet. thirty-seven, general health excellent until syphilis in 1894, was admitted to the Infirmary in 1898. He had had for two years recurrent attacks of paralysis of the external rectus muscle of the right eye, slight gastric crises, and stabbing pains in the legs; station very poor, but strength unimpaired, and he was able to walk after being a few minutes on his feet; when first rising he was very unsteady. Knee-jerk lost, no reinforcement. No sexual power. Some difficulty in emptying the bladder. Examination showed slight atrophy of both optic nerves, Argyll-Robertson pupil, and myosis. He was ordered two weeks' rest in bed, with massage, cool sponging daily, and galvanization of the areas of neuralgia. After two weeks he was allowed to get up gradually, to occupy himself as he pleased, but not to walk. Lessons in balance and co-ordination were begun in the fourth week of treatment, and supervised carefully for two weeks more. When his station and gait were both improved, he was permitted to walk, always with care not to fatigue himself. At this time, six weeks from commencement of treatment, his eyes were glassed by Dr. de Schweinitz. He had gained some pounds in weight, and walked on straight lines without noticeable incooerdination, but in turning short or walking sharp curves he was still unsteady. He found walking much easier than formerly and was less easily tired. After nine weeks he could stand or walk, even backward, with closed eyes. He was sent home for the summer, with directions to continue his co-ordination movements, to walk very little, and take such exercise as he needed on horseback, riding quietly. He had still some stabbing pains two or three times daily.

He reported in one month, and again in six months, "No improvement in the pains, but I walk well and briskly, can jump on a moving street-car, and have ridden a horse twenty miles in a day without fatigue."

This case was in one way favorable for treatment: the patient, an educated and intelligent man, helped in every way, carrying out minutely all orders, and had the good sense to begin treatment early. But the acuteness and rapidity of onset of the tabetic symptoms were so great that in a little more than two years they had reached a condition which most cases only attain in from five to ten years, and this makes the prognosis somewhat less favorable.

In the instance to be next related there was also antecedent syphilis, and the patient had already been heavily dosed with iodides and repeatedly salivated with mercury. His recovery was and has remained remarkably complete.

H.B., travelling salesman, from New York, aet. forty, single, a large, strongly-made man, a hard worker, given to excesses in sexual indulgence and alcohol for years. Syphilis was contracted fifteen years before the first traceable symptoms of ataxia, which had shown themselves after an attack of grippe, in 1890, in sudden remittent paralysis of the external muscles of the right eye, followed within a few months by gastric crises, general lightning pains appearing a few months later. During the two years succeeding he was drenched with drugs and grew steadily worse. When admitted to the hospital in 1892 he was very ataxic in the legs, suffered greatly from gastric and other pains, difficulties with bladder and rectum, loss of sexual power, various anaesthetic areas, could not stand with eyes open unless he had help, total loss of knee-jerk, paralysis of right rectus, indigestion from the ir- ritation of the stomach from medicines as well as from the disease, and, though muscular and over-fat, was flabby and pallid. He had no ataxia or loss of sensibility in the upper half of the body. He was in bed for two weeks, on milk diet, with warm baths and massage. Systematic movements were begun and massage continued. Af- ter the stomach improved he grew better with unusual rapidity. He is now able to work hard again, travels extensively, can walk strongly, but wisely takes his exer- cise more in the form of massage and systematic gymnastics. He appears to report himself once or twice a year. There has been a partial return of sexual ability.

The next case has points of interest in the later history, but the first examina- tions and early treatment may be passed over briefly. X.Y., aet. forty-two, a steady, sober merchant, closely confined by his business, always of excellent habits, with no possible suspicion of syphilis, was seen first in 1894 in a somewhat advanced stage of tabes, but with no optic or gastric disturbances. His station was very bad, but when once erect and started he could walk without a stick. Girdle-pains very marked; bowels very constipated; some trouble in emptying bladder; several points of fixed sharp pain; lightning pain occasional and severe, but not frequent. He was ordered to bed for six weeks. Galvanism, alternate hot- and cold-water applications to the tender spots, careful massage, and a two-months' course of Brown-Sequard fluid after getting up made a new man of him. Massage and systematic exercise were kept up together for six months. The massage was stopped and the exercises continued, and improvement went on steadily, though the fixed pains kept up in only slightly less severity.

In a year the patient was better in general health, looks, and spirits than he had been for many years before, and remained in good order, except for the daily recurrences of paroxysms of pain of varying but not unbearable severity for two years. He then presumed for a month on his strength, and took much more exercise afoot than was wise, worked late at night over his books, had some additional nervous strain from business worries, and came to Dr. J.K. Mitchell in October, 1898, barely able to crawl with two canes, having lost weight, become sleepless, suffered great increase of pain, and grown so ataxic that he could scarcely walk. This change had all occurred in three or four weeks. He became steadily worse for two or three weeks till he could not stand or walk at all, had cystitis from retention, violent attacks of rectal tenesmus, stabbing pains in rectum, perineum, scrotum, and groins, with almost total anaesthesia of the sacral region, buttocks, scrotum, and perineum, inability to retain faeces, while passages from the bowels took place without his knowledge. He found that an increase in the rectal and abdominal pain followed lying down. He therefore spent day and night sitting up. At the end of three weeks there was total paralysis of the legs, and the outlook seemed most unfavorable.

Massage was begun again, strychnia and salol were administered, and a short course of full doses of the testicular fluid was given. A rapidly interrupted faradic current, with an uncovered electrode, to the neighborhood of the rectum, bladder, and buttocks, greatly relieved the anaesthesia, upon which galvanism had no effect; and, in brief, from a state which looked almost as if the last paralytic stage of tabes had suddenly come upon him, he recovered in two months, and is now (July, 1899) better than he was a year ago, before the relapse, and will probably remain so, as he has had his warning.

Without multiplying case histories, it may be said that ataxic paraplegia (a combination of lateral and posterior sclerosis) may be treated in much the same manner. In this disease there is usually much less pain than in ataxia, but greater weakness, and late in its course some rigidity in the extensor groups of the legs; the knee-jerk is preserved or exaggerated. The disease is a rare one. But two recent distinct cases are in my list, and one of these, the one here reported, seems rather more like an ataxia with some anomalous symptoms. The second one had the symptom, uncommon in this malady, of very frequent and excessively severe stabbing pains, and though his co-ordination grew somewhat better, he improved very little in any other way, which, as his trouble was of fourteen years standing, was not astonishing.

The other patient, seen in 1897, was a rancher from New Mexico, thirty-three years old, who had led an active, hard-working, much-exposed life, but had been perfectly well until 1891, when he was said to have had an attack of spinal meningitis, from which he recovered very slowly. Four years later he noticed numbness of feet and weakness of legs, great enough to make it hard for him to get a leg over his horse. Some pains were felt in the limbs, and a constriction about the chest and abdomen, which had steadily increased in severity. Sharp attacks left distinct bruise-marks at the seat of pain each time. Could not empty bladder. Gait feeble, spastic, and paralytic, could not mount steps at all or stand without aid, sway very great. Knee-jerks and muscle-jerks increased, especially on left; ankle-clonus; very slight loss of touch-acuity in lower half of body. Eyes: muscles and eye-grounds negative; pupils equal and active. Bladder could not be emptied; cystitis. Ordered rest, massage, electricity, and full doses of iodide in skimmed milk. In this way he was able to take without distress or indigestion amounts as large as four hundred and forty grains a day. When education in balance, etc., was begun he could not walk without aid, or more than a few steps in any way. In three months from the time he went to bed he walked out-of-doors alone with no stick, and in five months went back to work. The bladder did not improve much until after regular washing out and intra-vesical galvanism were used, with full doses of strychnia. He was soon able to empty the organ twice a day, and since leaving the hospital writes that it gives him very little annoyance, though as a measure of precaution he uses a catheter once daily. His pains have entirely disappeared, and he is daily on horseback for many hours.

In spastic paralysis, whether in the slowly-developing forms in which it is seen in adults, due sometimes to multiple sclerosis, sometimes to brain tumor, sometimes following upon a transverse myelitis, or in the central paraplegia or diplegia of "birth-palsies," some very fortunate results have followed the careful application of the principles of treatment already described. Absolute confinement to bed is seldom required or in adults desirable, though exercise should be carefully limited to an amount which can be taken without fatigue, and some hours' rest lying down is usually advantageous.

Assuming that the necessary treatment for the disease originating the paralysis is to be carried on in the ordinary way, I will only describe the special forms and methods of exercise I have found serviceable. Whatever the cause, this will be much the same, though in birth-palsies the teaching may have to include groups of muscles and instruction in the co-ordination of actions which are not affected in adult subjects.

First, as to massage: the operator must direct his efforts primarily to the relaxation of the tense muscles, secondarily to the strengthening of the opponent groups, this last being of special importance where actual contraction has taken place. He should make frequent attempts by stretching the rigid groups to overcome the spasm, which in large muscle-masses may be done by grasping with both hands, taking care not to pinch, and pulling the hands apart in the line of the muscle's long axis, thus stretching the muscles. Pressure will sometimes accomplish the same end, and it will be found in certain cases that by kneading *during action*,--that is, while the patient endeavors to produce voluntary contraction,--the result will be better. Except in the most spastic states, a certain degree of relaxation is possible by effort, though not without practice, and this has to be constantly inculcated and encouraged. After a period varying in length according to the case, lessons in co-ordinating movements are begun. It is best for the patient's encouragement to start with the least affected muscles, so that, seeing the good results, he may be stimulated to persistent effort. The lessons differ only in detail from those given in the list under tabes. Improvement is slower than in ataxia.

In birth-palsy cases not much can be accomplished in the way of education, beyond the attempt by such means as ordinary gymnastics and lessons in drill and walking offer, until the child shall have reached an age when he is able to comprehend what is being attempted. For the imbecile, idiotic, or backward a training-school is the proper place, where mental and bodily functions may both receive attention and where constant intelligent supervision is available.

Many children the subjects of cerebral diplegia are credited with less intelligence than they really possess, partly because they are necessarily backward, and partly because of their difficulty in expressing themselves, the speech-muscles sharing in the disease. These muscles need to be carefully educated, and this might almost be made the subject of a treatise by itself. Each case will require study as to the special difficulties in the way of speech. Some experience most trouble with the vowel sounds, more find the consonants the worst obstacles. Patient practice in forming the sounds soon produce some results; the pupil must be taught, like the deaf mute, to watch and imitate the movements of the lips and tongue.

Seguin's books and the numerous special works should be consulted by the physician or parent desiring to pursue these methods to their fullest development.

When once the control of muscular movement begins to improve, more elaborate exercises may be set. In speech, if the patients be intelligent, they will sometimes be amused and profitably trained at the same time by the effort to learn and repeat long words or nonsensical combinations of difficult sounds, like the "Peter Piper" nursery rhymes.

B.M., aet. fourteen, an intelligent lad, of Jewish parentage, suffered a forceps-injury at birth, and had convulsive seizures later. He began to make futile attempts at walking when five or six years of age, when the spastic rigidity was first noticed. His speech was better at this time than later, and a sort of relapse seemed to be precipitated by a fall in which he struck his head when seven years of age. His mother, finding it almost impossible to teach him to walk, devoted herself faithfully to improving his mind, so that at fourteen years of age he read well and enjoyed books, and was mentally clear, observant, and docile. His speech was almost incomprehensible,--stuttering, thick, and nasal. He stood, swaying in every direction, though not apt to fall, with bent knees, rounded shoulders, every muscle in the extremities rigid, the mouth half-open, the head projected forward, and, upon attempting to move, the toes turned in, the legs almost twined around one another, and, unless supported, he would stumble and twist about, scarcely able to get forward at all. With a guiding hand he did a little better. His first lessons were in "setting-up drill," while the feeble, disused muscles were strengthened by massage, which served at the same time to help his very irritable and imperfect digestive apparatus, so that it was soon possible to give him a greater variety and more nourishing kinds of food than he had before been able to take. He was kept in bed up to three o'clock in the afternoon, the morning hours occupied with massage and a half-hour's lesson in erect standing, with slow trunk movements afterwards. An hour after dinner he was dressed and taken for two hours in a carriage or street-car. He did his reading and some study on his return, and had another half-hour's drill, superintended by his mother. In two or three weeks some improvement began to be observable in his attitude, and a great change in his color and general expression, but it was three months before it was thought wise to attempt education in small co-ordinate movements. At about the same time speech-drill was commenced.

In all these lessons the greatest care was taken that adequate rest should intervene between each series of efforts, and it was always found that fatigue distinctly impaired his co-ordination, as did emotion or indigestion. When his speech grew clearer he was set tasks of learning many-syllabled words and also began to practise drawing patterns. Every new lesson was first given under medical supervision and then continued by his mother or by the masseur. To shorten the history it will suffice to say that in six months he was able to go to school, where with certain allowances made for his thick speech by a kindly master he did well, and returned to his home in the South able to walk without attracting attention, to speak comprehensibly, to write a good letter, and with every prospect fair for a still greater improvement, which I learn he has since made.

The important things to be recognized in the treatment of these cases are, first, that rest in proper proportion allows of the patients doing an amount of exertion which, ungoverned, or performed in wrong ways would harm them; secondly, that full feeding is of value, because these disorders are mostly of the character of degenerations and involve failure of nutrition in various directions; and, lastly, that the exactness of routine is of the highest moral and mental as well as physical importance.

Paralysis agitans needs scarcely more than to be mentioned as amenable to the same methods, with small differences in the application of details. Body movements to counteract the tendency to rigidity in the flexor groups of spinal muscles will be especially useful, as the stiffness of these is one of the causes of displacement forward of the centre of gravity, a displacement which results in the festination symptom usually seen in such cases. Prescriptions of special exercises for the muscle-masses particularly involved in each instance must be given, remembering that contraction of the affected muscles will to a certain degree overcome their rigidity even at first, and to a still greater extent as the patient reacquires voluntary control.

INDEX.

NOTES:

[1: The Systematic Treatment of Nerve Prostration and Hysteria. London, 1883.]

[2: The Pennsylvania Orthopaedic Hospital and Infirmary for Diseases of the Nervous System.]

[3: Sur l'Homme, p. 47, et seq.]

[4: Growth of Children, p. 31.]

[5: See a valuable paper by Dr. Gerhard, Am. Jour. Med. Sci., 1876. Also Lectures on Diseases of the Nervous System, especially in Women. S. Weir Mitchell. Phila., 1881, p. 127. See also the papers by Dr. Morris J. Lewis on the seasonal relations of chorea, analyzing seven hundred and seventeen cases of chorea as to the months of onset (Trans. Assoc. Amer. Phys., 1892), and Osler On Chorea (1894).]

[6: Statistics (Anthropological) Surgeon-General's Bureau--1875.]

[7: This excess of corpulence in the English is attained chiefly after forty, as I have said. The average American is taller than the average Englishman, and is fully as well built in proportion to his height, as Gould has shown. The child of either sex in New England is both taller and heavier than the English child of corresponding class and age, as Dr. H.I. Bowditch has lately made clear; while the English of the manufacturing and agricultural classes are miserably inferior to the members of a similar class in America.]

[8: Zeitschrift fuer Biol., 1872. Phila. Med. Times, vol. iii., page 115.]

[9: Letheby on Food, pp. 39, 40, 41.]

[10: Am. Jour. Med. Sci.; Proc. Phil. Coll. of Phys., 1883; Phil. Med. News, April, 1883.]

[11: Chorea. See Lancet, Aug. 1882.]

[12: "Nurse and Patient." S. Weir Mitchell. Lippincott's Magazine, Dec. 1872.]

[13: See Philip Karell's remarks on the use of treatment by milk in cardiac hypertrophy. Edin. Med. Jour., Aug. 1866.]

[14: Trans. Obst. Soc. of London, vol. xxxiii.]

[15: Seguin Lecture, *op. cit.*]

[16: "Pinch" is used to avoid the use of a technical term, but should be understood to mean the grasping and squeezing of a part with the whole hand, using the palmar portion of the fingers to press the grasped mass against the "heel" of the hand. Fuller technical details of the massage process and consideration of its effects will be found in the excellent "Handbook" of Kleen, in the works of Dr. Douglas Graham, Dr. A. Symon Eccles, and in an article in Professor Clifford Albutt's "System of Medicine" (1896), by Dr. John K. Mitchell.]

[17: Dr. Symon Eccles in "The Practice of Massage" recommends this order.]

[18: Some care is needed not to overwork patients. For details I must refer to manuals of Swedish Gymnastics.]

[19: See also page 91.]

[20: A number of observations in late years have been made upon the effect of massage upon elimination. Among the articles to which the practitioner desiring further to study this subject may be referred are,--

Edin. Clin. and Path. Jour., Aug., 1884.

Jour, of Physiol., vol. xxii., p. 68.

Centralbl. f. Inner. Med., 1894, No. 40, p. 944.

Munch. Med. Woch., April 11 and April 18, 1899 (Influence of bodily exercise upon temperature in health and disease).

Numerous articles by Mosso, Arbelous, W. Bain, Lauder-Brunton, Lepicque and Marette, and Maggiora.]

[21: American Journal of the Medical Sciences, May, 1894.]

[22: Numerous examinations made since have quite uniformly agreed with the former remarkably constant results.]

[23: J.K. Mitchell, *loc. cit.*]

[24: Most induction batteries are without any arrangement for making infrequent breaks in the current.]

[25: In the extreme constipation of certain hysterical women, good may be done by placing one conductor in the rectum and moving the other over the abdomen so as to cause full movement of the muscles. This means must at first be employed cautiously, and the amount of electricity carefully increased. It is doubtful if any movement of the intestinal muscle-fibres is thus caused, but that it is a useful method of stimulation in obstinate cases may be taken as proved.]

[26: Harvey on Corpulence.]

[27: The management of the morphia or chloral habit becomes much more easy under a milk diet, massage, and absolute rest, and I can with confidence commend their use in these difficult cases. Massage in the morning is liked, and general surface-rubbing without muscle-kneading at night very often proves remarkably soothing, while the rest in bed cuts off many opportunities to indulge in the temptation to secure the desired drugs.]

[28: I have found that this may be usefully replaced by one of the numerous peptonized foods described in the pamphlets issued by the manufacturers of the peptonizing powders. The ready-made peptonized preparations vary very much, like some of the beef extracts, but a trial will discover which of them is best fitted for an individual case.]

[29: Nerve Prostration and Hysteria.]

[30: It is worth mentioning that where ataxic patients have to use canes, a crutch-cane with a base some six or eight inches long and well shod with roughened rubber is far more useful and safer than the ordinary stick.]

www.bookjungle.com *email: sales@bookjungle.com fax: 630-214-0564 mail: Book Jungle PO Box 2226 Champaign, IL 61825*

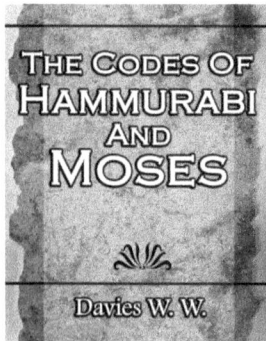

The Codes Of Hammurabi And Moses
W. W. Davies

QTY

The discovery of the Hammurabi Code is one of the greatest achievements of archaeology, and is of paramount interest, not only to the student of the Bible, but also to all those interested in ancient history...

Religion   **ISBN:** *1-59462-338-4*

Pages:132

MSRP $12.95

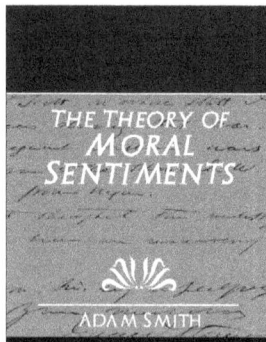

The Theory of Moral Sentiments
Adam Smith

QTY

This work from 1749. contains original theories of conscience amd moral judgment and it is the foundation for systemof morals.

Philosophy   **ISBN:** *1-59462-777-0*

Pages:536

MSRP $19.95

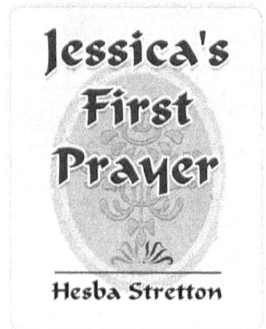

Jessica's First Prayer
Hesba Stretton

QTY

In a screened and secluded corner of one of the many railway-bridges which span the streets of London there could be seen a few years ago, from five o'clock every morning until half past eight, a tidily set-out coffee-stall, consisting of a trestle and board, upon which stood two large tin cans, with a small fire of charcoal burning under each so as to keep the coffee boiling during the early hours of the morning when the work-people were thronging into the city on their way to their daily toil...

Childrens   **ISBN:** *1-59462-373-2*

Pages:84

MSRP $9.95

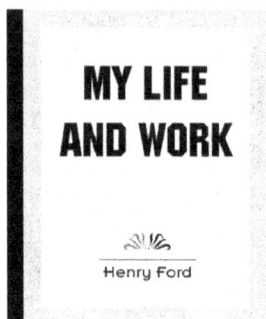

My Life and Work
Henry Ford

QTY

Henry Ford revolutionized the world with his implementation of mass production for the Model T automobile. Gain valuable business insight into his life and work with his own auto-biography... "We have only started on our development of our country we have not as yet, with all our talk of wonderful progress, done more than scratch the surface. The progress has been wonderful enough but..."

Biographies/   **ISBN:** *1-59462-198-5*

Pages:300

MSRP $21.95

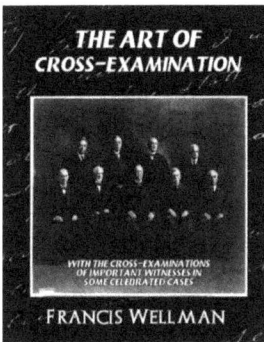

The Art of Cross-Examination
Francis Wellman

QTY

I presume it is the experience of every author, after his first book is published upon an important subject, to be almost overwhelmed with a wealth of ideas and illustrations which could readily have been included in his book, and which to his own mind, at least, seem to make a second edition inevitable. Such certainly was the case with me; and when the first edition had reached its sixth impression in five months, I rejoiced to learn that it seemed to my publishers that the book had met with a sufficiently favorable reception to justify a second and considerably enlarged edition. ..

Reference   ISBN: *1-59462-647-2*

Pages:412

MSRP $19.95

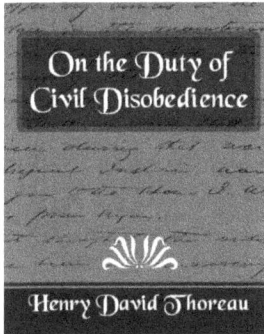

On the Duty of Civil Disobedience
Henry David Thoreau

QTY

Thoreau wrote his famous essay, On the Duty of Civil Disobedience, as a protest against an unjust but popular war and the immoral but popular institution of slave-owning. He did more than write—he declined to pay his taxes, and was hauled off to gaol in consequence. Who can say how much this refusal of his hastened the end of the war and of slavery ?

Law   ISBN: *1-59462-747-9*

Pages:48

MSRP $7.45

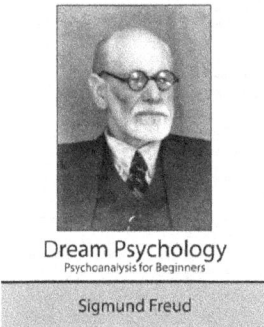

Dream Psychology Psychoanalysis for Beginners
Sigmund Freud

QTY

Sigmund Freud, born Sigismund Schlomo Freud (May 6, 1856 - September 23, 1939), was a Jewish-Austrian neurologist and psychiatrist who co-founded the psychoanalytic school of psychology. Freud is best known for his theories of the unconscious mind, especially involving the mechanism of repression; his redefinition of sexual desire as mobile and directed towards a wide variety of objects; and his therapeutic techniques, especially his understanding of transference in the therapeutic relationship and the presumed value of dreams as sources of insight into unconscious desires.

Psychology   ISBN: *1-59462-905-6*

Pages:196

MSRP $15.45

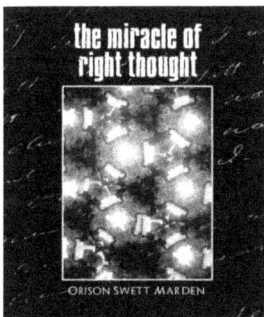

The Miracle of Right Thought
Orison Swett Marden

QTY

Believe with all of your heart that you will do what you were made to do. When the mind has once formed the habit of holding cheerful, happy, prosperous pictures, it will not be easy to form the opposite habit. It does not matter how improbable or how far away this realization may see, or how dark the prospects may be, if we visualize them as best we can, as vividly as possible, hold tenaciously to them and vigorously struggle to attain them, they will gradually become actualized, realized in the life. But a desire, a longing without endeavor, a yearning abandoned or held indifferently will vanish without realization.

Pages:360

Self Help   ISBN: *1-59462-644-8*

MSRP $25.45

The Rosicrucian Cosmo-Conception Mystic Christianity *by Max Heindel*   ISBN: *1-59462-188-8*   **$38.95**
The Rosicrucian Cosmo-conception is not dogmatic, neither does it appeal to any other authority than the reason of the student. It is: not controversial, but is: sent forth in the, hope that it may help to clear...   New Age/Religion Pages 646

Abandonment To Divine Providence *by Jean-Pierre de Caussade*   ISBN: *1-59462-228-0*   **$25.95**
"The Rev. Jean Pierre de Caussade was one of the most remarkable spiritual writers of the Society of Jesus in France in the 18th Century. His death took place at Toulouse in 1751. His works have gone through many editions and have been republished...   Inspirational/Religion Pages 400

Mental Chemistry *by Charles Haanel*   ISBN: *1-59462-192-6*   **$23.95**
Mental Chemistry allows the change of material conditions by combining and appropriately utilizing the power of the mind. Much like applied chemistry creates something new and unique out of careful combinations of chemicals the mastery of mental chemistry...   New Age Pages 354

The Letters of Robert Browning and Elizabeth Barret Barrett 1845-1846 vol II   ISBN: *1-59462-193-4*   **$35.95**
by Robert Browning and Elizabeth Barrett   Biographies Pages 596

Gleanings In Genesis (volume I) *by Arthur W. Pink*   ISBN: *1-59462-130-6*   **$27.45**
Appropriately has Genesis been termed "the seed plot of the Bible" for in it we have, in germ form, almost all of the great doctrines which are afterwards fully developed in the books of Scripture which follow...   Religion/Inspirational Pages 420

The Master Key *by L. W. de Laurence*   ISBN: *1-59462-001-6*   **$30.95**
In no branch of human knowledge has there been a more lively increase of the spirit of research during the past few years than in the study of Psychology, Concentration and Mental Discipline. The requests for authentic lessons in Thought Control, Mental Discipline and...   New Age/Business Pages 422

The Lesser Key Of Solomon Goetia *by L. W. de Laurence*   ISBN: *1-59462-092-X*   **$9.95**
This translation of the first book of the "Lernegton" which is now for the first time made accessible to students of Talismanic Magic was done, after careful collation and edition, from numerous Ancient Manuscripts in Hebrew, Latin, and French...   New Age/Occult Pages 92

Rubaiyat Of Omar Khayyam *by Edward Fitzgerald*   ISBN:*1-59462-332-5*   **$13.95**
Edward Fitzgerald, whom the world has already learned, in spite of his own efforts to remain within the shadow of anonymity, to look upon as one of the rarest poets of the century, was born at Bredfield, in Suffolk, on the 31st of March, 1809. He was the third son of John Purcell...   Music Pages 172

Ancient Law *by Henry Maine*   ISBN: *1-59462-128-4*   **$29.95**
The chief object of the following pages is to indicate some of the earliest ideas of mankind, as they are reflected in Ancient Law, and to point out the relation of those ideas to modern thought.   Religiom/History Pages 452

Far-Away Stories *by William J. Locke*   ISBN: *1-59462-129-2*   **$19.45**
"Good wine needs no bush, but a collection of mixed vintages does. And this book is just such a collection. Some of the stories I do not want to remain buried for ever in the museum files of dead magazine-numbers an author's not unpardonable vanity..."   Fiction Pages 272

Life of David Crockett *by David Crockett*   ISBN: *1-59462-250-7*   **$27.45**
"Colonel David Crockett was one of the most remarkable men of the times in which he lived. Born in humble life, but gifted with a strong will, an indomitable courage, and unremitting perseverance...   Biographies/New Age Pages 424

Lip-Reading *by Edward Nitchie*   ISBN: *1-59462-206-X*   **$25.95**
Edward B. Nitchie, founder of the New York School for the Hard of Hearing, now the Nitchie School of Lip-Reading, Inc, wrote "LIP-READING Principles and Practice". The development and perfecting of this meritorious work on lip-reading was an undertaking...   How-to Pages 400

A Handbook of Suggestive Therapeutics, Applied Hypnotism, Psychic Science   ISBN: *1-59462-214-0*   **$24.95**
by Henry Munro   Health/New Age/Health/Self-help Pages 376

A Doll's House: and Two Other Plays *by Henrik Ibsen*   ISBN: *1-59462-112-8*   **$19.95**
Henrik Ibsen created this classic when in revolutionary 1848 Rome. Introducing some striking concepts in playwriting for the realist genre, this play has been studied the world over.   Fiction/Classics/Plays 308

The Light of Asia *by sir Edwin Arnold*   ISBN: *1-59462-204-3*   **$13.95**
In this poetic masterpiece, Edwin Arnold describes the life and teachings of Buddha. The man who was to become known as Buddha to the world was born as Prince Gautama of India but he rejected the worldly riches and abandoned the reigns of power when...   Religion/History/Biographies Pages 170

The Complete Works of Guy de Maupassant *by Guy de Maupassant*   ISBN: *1-59462-157-8*   **$16.95**
"For days and days, nights and nights, I had dreamed of that first kiss which was to consecrate our engagement, and I knew not on what spot I should put my lips..."   Fiction/Classics Pages 240

The Art of Cross-Examination *by Francis L. Wellman*   ISBN: *1-59462-309-0*   **$26.95**
Written by a renowned trial lawyer, Wellman imparts his experience and uses case studies to explain how to use psychology to extract desired information through questioning.   How-to/Science/Reference Pages 408

Answered or Unanswered? *by Louisa Vaughan*   ISBN: *1-59462-248-5*   **$10.95**
Miracles of Faith in China   Religion Pages 112

The Edinburgh Lectures on Mental Science (1909) *by Thomas*   ISBN: *1-59462-008-3*   **$11.95**
This book contains the substance of a course of lectures recently given by the writer in the Queen Street Hail, Edinburgh. Its purpose is to indicate the Natural Principles governing the relation between Mental Action and Material Conditions...   New Age/Psychology Pages 148

Ayesha *by H. Rider Haggard*   ISBN: *1-59462-301-5*   **$24.95**
Verily and indeed it is the unexpected that happens! Probably if there was one person upon the earth from whom the Editor of this, and of a certain previous history, did not expect to hear again...   Classics Pages 380

Ayala's Angel *by Anthony Trollope*   ISBN: *1-59462-352-X*   **$29.95**
The two girls were both pretty, but Lucy who was twenty-one who supposed to be simple and comparatively unattractive, whereas Ayala was credited, as her Bombwhat romantic name might show, with poetic charm and a taste for romance. Ayala when her father died was nineteen...   Fiction Pages 484

The American Commonwealth *by James Bryce*   ISBN: *1-59462-286-8*   **$34.45**
An interpretation of American democratic political theory. It examines political mechanics and society from the perspective of Scotsman James Bryce   Politics Pages 572

Stories of the Pilgrims *by Margaret P. Pumphrey*   ISBN: *1-59462-116-0*   **$17.95**
This book explores pilgrims religious oppression in England as well as their escape to Holland and eventual crossing to America on the Mayflower, and their early days in New England...   History Pages 268

QTY

The Fasting Cure *by Sinclair Upton* ISBN: *1-59462-222-1* **$13.95**
In the Cosmopolitan Magazine for May, 1910, and in the Contemporary Review (London) for April, 1910, I published an article dealing with my experiences in fasting. I have written a great many magazine articles, but never one which attracted so much attention... New Age/Self Help/Health Pages 164

Hebrew Astrology *by Sepharial* ISBN: *1-59462-308-2* **$13.45**
In these days of advanced thinking it is a matter of common observation that we have left many of the old landmarks behind and that we are now pressing forward to greater heights and to a wider horizon than that which represented the mind-content of our progenitors... Astrology Pages 144

Thought Vibration or The Law of Attraction in the Thought World ISBN: *1-59462-127-6* **$12.95**
by William Walker Atkinson Psychology/Religion Pages 144

Optimism *by Helen Keller* ISBN: *1-59462-108-X* **$15.95**
Helen Keller was blind, deaf, and mute since 19 months old, yet famously learned how to overcome these handicaps, communicate with the world, and spread her lectures promoting optimism. An inspiring read for everyone... Biographies/Inspirational Pages 84

Sara Crewe *by Frances Burnett* ISBN: *1-59462-360-0* **$9.45**
In the first place, Miss Minchin lived in London. Her home was a large, dull, tall one, in a large, dull square, where all the houses were alike, and all the sparrows were alike, and where all the door-knockers made the same heavy sound... Childrens/Classic Pages 88

The Autobiography of Benjamin Franklin *by Benjamin Franklin* ISBN: *1-59462-135-7* **$24.95**
The Autobiography of Benjamin Franklin has probably been more extensively read than any other American historical work, and no other book of its kind has had such ups and downs of fortune. Franklin lived for many years in England, where he was agent... Biographies/History Pages 332

Name	
Email	
Telephone	
Address	
City, State ZIP	

☐ **Credit Card**   ☐ **Check / Money Order**

Credit Card Number	
Expiration Date	
Signature	

Please Mail to: Book Jungle
PO Box 2226
Champaign, IL 61825
or Fax to: 630-214-0564

ORDERING INFORMATION

web*: www.bookjungle.com*
email*: sales@bookjungle.com*
fax*: 630-214-0564*
mail*: Book Jungle PO Box 2226 Champaign, IL 61825*
or PayPal *to sales@bookjungle.com*

Please contact us for bulk discounts

DIRECT-ORDER TERMS

**20% Discount if You Order
Two or More Books**
Free Domestic Shipping!
Accepted: Master Card, Visa,
Discover, American Express

www.ingramcontent.com/pod-product-compliance
Lightning Source LLC
LaVergne TN
LVHW061225060426
835509LV00012B/1422